Endorsements for *Mercy Extended*

Linda Oberbrunner has walked the talk and has lived a life of extended mercy to all she knows. Her words are trusted, her life lived by example, her heart is true, her purpose God-orientated. A must read as we all need *Mercy Extended*!

—Wendy Gebauer, Adoption Paralegal

My wife and I met Linda during the adoption of our son, Tommy. She is an amazing woman as you will see through this book. Linda has exemplified faith and obedience throughout her ministry. It seems like every time she becomes comfortable, God brings a new challenge which may seem daunting but which she ultimately embraces with faith and enthusiasm. Linda has been a gift from God to Debbie and me as you will see why when you read *Mercy Extended*.

—Brian McIntyre, Director of
West African Mercy Ministries

Reading *Mercy Extended* was like traveling through a parallel universe … Linda Oberbrunner's and my own. That's what mercy is like—always unique yet so very common. Thank you, Linda, for allowing us all to remember, for just a moment, our own remarkable past. And thank you also for exalting the Lord as your writing brings to life the truth that "mercy there was great, and grace was free …"

—Frederick Smith, Pastor, Attorney,
Public Servant, & Friend

I finished your book in two nights! What a blessing you and your book are and will be to those who read it. I was moved to tears dozens of times when reading the precious stories that you shared about God's mercy in your life and other's lives too.

—Julie West, Relationship Program Manager,
Colgate-Palmolive Company

In a fresh and transparent way, Linda opens her heart for the reader to see and experience her life, as God in His Mercy goes before her. This is a captivating book by a humble servant whose life points people to Jesus Christ so they also can know His Mercy Extended intimately.

—Jim Valentine, Past Chairman ECFA Advisory Council,
Cousins Subs Restaurants Franchisee

Mercy Extended is aptly titled and is authored by someone who definitely has and beautifully uses the gift of mercy. Using her own unique life story, Linda shows how God extends mercy to us even before we know Him and even when we don't understand what He's up to. With an openness that is both rare and refreshing and with great touches of humor just when we need them, Linda relates the good and sad experiences she's been part of, all with an eye extolling our merciful God and urging us to join her in looking every day for how God has been merciful to us and for ways we can extend mercy to those around us.

—Julaine Appling, President of Wisconsin Family Council;
also an earthly and heavenly daughter by the grace
and mercy of adoption

The spiritual gift of mercy presents so many opportunities to minister and share the love of God. *Mercy Extended* provides inspirational, true stories that will help you to become a vessel of mercy and influence the lives of people who need Jesus and the body of Christ alike. Author Linda Oberbrunner clearly explains how God can use anyone who lets the mercy of God flow through them and enables us to show mercy to others.

—Paul van Gorkom, Executive Director, GoServ Global

As one of Linda's partner professionals when she was at Evangelical Child and Family Agency, I witnessed the mercy Linda extended to our clients who were experiencing crisis pregnancy. Mercy was expressed in compassion and care to mothers who were considering ending the life of their unborn children. This mercy flowed from Linda's deep understanding of her Savior's love for her. The hurting mothers who were assisted made life decisions that impacted a generation yet to be born.

—Dottie Enters, Executive Director,
Eyewitness for Life, Ltd

To truly understand mercy, don't read its cold definition in a dictionary. Instead, take a journey with Linda Oberbrunner in her book *Mercy Extended* and learn about its transformative power. With each page and compelling story, you will be drawn in and filled with compassion for others in a new way.

—Skip Prichard, CEO, Speaker, Wall Street Journal
Bestselling Author of *The Book of Mistakes:*
9 Secrets to Creating a Successful Future

Linda has been a dear friend for many years and a great source of encouragement to me in my journey to minister to foster and adoptive families. God has extended an abundance of mercy to Mike and Linda over the years but has also worked through them by touching so many with God's mercy. *Mercy Extended* challenges us to see mercy and extend mercy in the ordinary parts of our lives and be reminded that we have a Savior who loves us unconditionally!

—Karen Schlindwein, Vice President of Education/ Development, Chosen, Inc., and Co-author of *Dear Lois: Our Adoption Journey.*

I worked with Linda in her various careers while I was a Waukesha, Wisconsin, Police Officer. With a huge smile and warm heart, Linda has traveled God's journey through life—delivering mercy, compassion, love, and kindness to those she encountered. These true stories show the true greatness of the world we live in!

—Lieutenant Billy Graham (retired) Waukesha, WI. Police Department (1969-2009)

In this riveting, real-life journey, Linda Oberbrunner brings a fresh understanding of how to gratefully live, deeply experience, and continually bask in God's amazing mercies. Around every corner, mercy shows up. Delightful! Captivating! Engaging! A must-read as we navigate the uncertainty of everyday life.

—Margo Fieseler, Author *Unwavering: Learning to Do the Next Right Thing in Your Walk With God,* Speaker, Expository Bible Teacher, Radio Personality, President of Margo Fieseler Ministries, Inc.

The quest to know Jesus Christ and serve Him is an adventure to behold. Working with the weak, downtrodden, orphans, and young girls in need of help is the story of Linda's life and her desire to do it in the mercy and grace of God. She experienced God's grace in her life and delights to share with it with others. This book will challenge you to demonstrate it in your own life.

—John Duckhorn, Bible Teacher, Former Pastoral Consultant for Evangelical Child & Family Agency, Missionary

God's throne of old where He met with His people was called the mercy seat. In Hebrews Chapter Four, we are told to come boldly to God's throne of grace. Why? So that we may receive mercy and find grace to help us in our time of need. Each and every one of us are in desperate need of God's mercy. *Mercy Extended* clearly shows the lasting impact that God's amazing mercy can have on each and every one who experience it. As you read of mercy being extended to others, it will renew your excitement to be involved in spreading this life-changing gift of God's mercy! Thank you so much, Linda, for sharing your own story of God's mercy in your life and for introducing us to so many champions of mercy. And thank you for being one yourself!

—Matt & Angie Hall, Bible Translators/Missionary Coaches in Papua New Guinea with Ethnos 360

MERCY
EXTENDED

MERCY EXTENDED

The Gift that Transforms Lives,
Impacts Generations, and Mobilizes
Multitudes for Eternity

LINDA OBERBRUNNER

Published by Author Academy Elite
PO Box 43, Powell, OH 43065
www.AuthorAcademyElite.com

Identifiers:

LCCN: 2020904369
ISBN: 978-1-64746-182-9 (paperback)
ISBN: 978-1-64746-183-6 (hardback)
ISBN: 978-1-64746-184-3 (ebook)

Available in paperback, hardback, e-book, and audiobook.

Cover design by Debbie O'Byrne.

DEDICATION

The book is dedicated first and foremost
to God, the FATHER of all mercies

&

My dad,
Daniel J. Schatzman, who taught me by example
the depth of mercy extended

MERCY EXTENDED

The Gift that Transforms Lives, Impacts Generations,
and Mobilizes Multitudes for Eternity

THANK YOU!

A portion of the proceeds from each book is donated to West African Mercy Ministries—WestAfricanMercy.org

COVER DESIGN CREDIT & COMMENTARY

This intricately detailed charcoal drawing of a newborn baby was chosen for the cover of this book to convey the title and essence of *Mercy Extended*. In 2015, our oldest daughter, Kim, was walking through a night market in Thailand admiring the craftsmanship of rural artisans. She was drawn to the space of one local Thai who had a few of his drawings on display in a rudimentary setting.

As she wandered, her attention was captured by the tender drawing of masculine hands enfolding and supporting the tiny infant. She decided at the moment to purchase the sketch as a gift. It would be saved, then given in the event I'd choose to retire from my beloved position. At that time, I was working with birth moms and dads in unplanned pregnancies along with adoption and foster care families.

In October 2017, after flying twenty-two hours to Wisconsin from her home in southeast Asia, Kim presented the framed drawing from all of our adult children—Kary, Sarah, and Jeremy (JJ)—who gathered for my retirement party from Evangelical Child & Family Agency (ECFA).

The drawing, created by an unknown artist, was and remains a priceless reminder today of the loving, merciful Father in heaven who desires to cradle me and you.

♥ Linda

FOREWORD

In 2018, my mom asked if we needed any volunteers at our annual Igniting Souls Conference. Since our business was growing faster than any of us could manage, I enthusiastically agreed. Never knowing a stranger, I knew my mom would excel in any area where she would interface with people.

The team picked her to oversee the conference bookstore. Although our event is designed for coaches, speakers, and entrepreneurs, most attendees are also authors. The entire weekend, she loved on these authors, making sure their books were adequately stocked and attractively displayed.

She heard hundreds of these authors tell their distinct story of how their books were strategically positioned in the marketplace and the ministry to impact others worldwide. Listening intently to their stories, she encouraged each one in their unique journey. As the conference came to an end, Martyn Wood, a long-time client, approached her. He said the Holy Spirit led him to pray for her and the success of her ministry told through her future book.

Although she hadn't thought of writing a book, she couldn't shake Martyn's prayer. Since her professional career in social work and director of the Wisconsin Evangelical Family Agency ended the year before, she now had the time to write that book.

When she told me her desire, I rejoiced with her. I love publishing people's dreams, and I never thought I'd have the honor of publishing one of my family members, not to mention my own mother.

We immediately enrolled her in our program, and she started Author Academy Elite with passionate determination. It was special coaching my mom on some of our author calls. With each passing week, I could see her book taking shape.

I tell people that writing a book will change you as a person. In my mom's case, this was especially true. Although writing the book took her longer than expected, it also led her into places physically, emotionally, and spiritually she never would have expected.

A few months into the book-writing process, she told our family she wanted to visit a mission in Africa for research purposes related to the book. As a grandmother in her sixties, she made the international trip with the mindset and enthusiasm of a twenty-year-old. She also reconnected with past clients, friends, and ministry partners throughout the writing process.

My dad supported my mom every step of the way, even attending the Igniting Souls Conference the following year. Together, they served in the conference bookstore. Our family was amazed at how my introverted dad became the talk of the conference as the kind, outgoing encourager. He even tied a tie for one of the male authors on the night of the Author Academy Awards.

He emerged from that experience convinced every person alive has a book inside them. My dad will tell you not everyone is able to write the book, but everyone has a story worth telling. (This is often where collaborators and ghostwriters come in at times, to assist with the writing process.)

In the fall of 2019, my mom's health suffered due to unknown reasons. By this time, her book was mostly written. In the next few months, she shared the manuscript with me, and through reading it, I had the honor of getting to know her, her childhood, and my deceased grandparents.

The experience was incredibly rewarding. I now have a much richer understanding of my past and the deep legacy forged by previous generations.

In these pages, you will encounter a rare story of God's grace and goodness. You'll see how mercy triumphs and confounds the wisdom of this world. And mostly, you'll have the choice to respond to the *Mercy Extended* to you in the person of Jesus Christ, God's gift to a world in desperate need of good news.

Enjoy this true story of imperfect humans finding the God who made them. If you read it with an open mind, I know you'll experience a changed heart.

—Kary Oberbrunner, author of *Your Secret Name* and *The Deeper Path*, CEO of Author Academy Elite, and even more significant, son of Mike and Linda Oberbrunner

NOTE TO THE READER

Evidently, there has been a theme running throughout my life that I have only recently begun to recognize as intentionally designed. Taking the time to piece together childhood recollections, true stories, and real-life heroes from various decades in my life, I've discovered how they seamlessly fall into place collectively under the same topic. This hidden thread I've evidently ignored for quite some time has been my lifelong companion. I'm finally ready to acknowledge this subject and am excited to share what I have learned with joy and heartache too. In reality, it has been the very root of my life's passion. It's a two-syllable word comprised of only five letters: M–E–R–C–Y. In all my tomorrows, I will continue to learn something new— and someday, I know I will live relishing the eternal value of this gift as an undeserved receiver.

In my earlier years, **mercy** was misdefined. As a young adult, **mercy** became *manifested*. When I willingly embraced additional roles in life, **mercy** *materialized*. And through numerous seasons and valued connections, **mercy** continues to be *mobilized*.

Ironically, this micro-sized word has provided me with an ample abundance of material, stories, analogies, and memories to share. In fact, there was enough to write an entire fourteen-chapter-plus book that can technically be read by you, my treasured reader, in a short amount of time. This last statement is only true, however, if you place limits on your eating, drinking, sleeping, relationships, and exercise. Then, further decide upon setting restrictive intake, output, position, isolation, cell-phone shutdown, muscle-tone neglect, and limitation of boundary square footage to only a few survival options.

Continuing on to turn the next page is definitely your decision. It is my deepest desire to provide you with a valuable experience that does not end with the last chapter. So, my new forever friend, accept the deepest thanks from my heart for beginning this time together.

PART ONE

MERCY MISDEFINED

1

MODELED

Do you remember the first time someone read you a story? Not any story, but one that stirred emotions in you of curiosity, compassion, and care? The textured covers of the book that surrounded the worn pages you never tired from hearing over and over? Even the smell of that book elicited a smile. I vividly remember with deep fondness the beloved reader, my dad. His appropriate voice inflections distinguished between the animal and human characters. The colorful pages of animated illustrations enraptured my attention since I could not decipher the printed words on each page as a young child. It was the telling and retelling of this story that slowly began a lifetime call.

Each night as the sun began to set, I looked forward to hearing the sound of the backdoor opening coupled with my dad's warm announcement to my mom and two of us littles, "Sweetie, Lindy & Danny, I'm hoommme." He returned each evening at right around the same time from working as a well-loved salesman in the office equipment business. I was only three years old, and my brother was barely two, only thirteen months younger than me. We both had wispy naturally wavy white-blonde hair. Mine tangled easily overnight and presented quite a challenge for my mom to brush and comb every morning. My brother's hair was kept short, making it easy to brush and slick over to the side. Both of us had blankets we were quite attached to that we affectionately named. Mine was "Kitty," and my brother's was "Ricky."

When we heard our dad's voice, we'd squeal with delight and grab our blankets, running as fast as we could for our group squeeze—but only after my mom received hers first, a hug combined with a tender kiss. Then, it was our turn to be firmly hugged by Dad while my mom left the circle for only a minute. She returned shortly, clenching my favorite book, which she handed to my dad. Meanwhile, Danny and I postured ourselves on an overstuffed couch clutching Kitty and Ricky, respectively. A corner from our blankets would drape strategically across our right thumbs, which were ready for occasionally sucking during the scary part of the book. My mom retreated to the kitchen to complete the dinner preparations for all of us, and I imagine she also enjoyed some quiet moments to herself.

My interest in my life's work was kindled at a young age, ironically, by a book now considered politically incorrect. This personally beloved life-impacting book by Helen Bannerman published in 1925 by The Platt and Munk Company of New York was called *Little Black Sambo*. I nearly had this version memorized by age four as my dad patiently read the storyline repeatedly. My brother was not as big a fan of this book, and after a few months, he shared his displeasure through what would be termed now as a justified meltdown. Sensitively, my dad switched off to reading aloud from a Golden Book in a generationally approved series, which included *The Poky Little Puppy*,

The Little Red Hen, and *Saggy Baggy Elephant.* Any one of those three titles captured Danny's full attention and my half-hearted interest.

By today's standards, that favored version of *Little Black Sambo* may be considered offensive, legitimately unsafe to read to some traumatized adults, and positively politically incorrect. In no way am I diminishing the feelings of today's readers, but please understand that many years ago, this book was the perfect means used to ignite a passion in me to become merciful to others. In fact, it was originally written by a nurturing mother with the intent to bring enjoyment to her own children. However, as the years passed and the norms and culture changed, the book was banned in many countries and was rewritten, revised, re-illustrated, and reintroduced over and over again.

In the story, the main human characters comprised a family of three—the father, Black Jumbo; the mother, Black Mumbo; and their young son, Little Black Sambo. They lived together in a jungle land far, far away where tigers freely dwelt and spoke. (My dad told me the land was Africa, although the author may have told her children it was India, though not specified.) One day, Little Black Sambo's parents gave him some special presents. His mother made some of them, and his father purchased the others. Sambo was so happy with his presents that he put them on to show off to anyone in the jungle whom he might meet by chance as he walked all by himself.

Unexpectedly, he encountered four tigers all at separate intervals. Each time he met with another tiger, they spoke to him in his same language. Each was very mean, selfish, demanding, fierce, and prideful. Yet Little Black Sambo responded with mercy to each even though all of his presents became the property of the tigers. Their pride led to uncontrollable jealously and eventually their unusual demise as a group. This was followed by a large high-calorie breakfast for the family of three and even the return of Little Black Sambo's presents. They seemed to all live happily ever after (although not actually stated).

If you are familiar with that fable, then you may have lots of memories resurfacing that are wide and varied. Correct? And if you were unfamiliar with the title and brief summary, you may have many questions that are varied or have piqued your curiosity.

My parents unknowingly used this book to reach my three-year-old heart. Up until age three, I only interacted with members of my family, my extended family of two grandmas, one grandpa, my chosen godparents—Aunt Marion aka "Aunt Mike" and Uncle Clarence aka "Huntz"—special aunts and uncles, second cousins all older but kind, a few of my parent's friends that played cards, an occasional babysitter, my next door neighbor best friends Pat and Mike and their parents, a priest, a few nuns, and the milkman (yes, a delivery guy who came every few days to drop off fresh milk and pick up the empty milk bottles). Thanks for humoring me through the list. The reason I shared the detail was that the one thing in common was that every face no matter what the age—wrinkled, freckled, or smooth, glasses, or not—everyone I knew in my life was light-skinned, as in white American. That is until one day when *Little Black Sambo* was read to me, and my life began to change.

It started with page observations, comparisons, and then light bulbs going off in my brain. Gradually, additional questions surfaced that were met with temporary satisfaction. A final question combined with a request was posed. "Daddy, will I ever get to meet someone with skin that is different than mine?" I still remember being positively assured by my own father (who never broke his word) that he would make this become a reality. In my mind, I wondered how and when this might happen, and I still recall how he responded. He told me stories of when he was little and played with children in his neighborhood that had other skin shades. His accounts made me want to start school that moment to see if I could duplicate his experience but would have to wait for at least another year. He also shared stories of being in the Army and meeting other men from all over the world. His personal stories became almost as exciting as Little Black Sambo's adventure. My brother, Danny, however, still preferred hearing the *Poky Little Puppy*, hoping we might someday become pet owners.

My mom became pregnant again and delivered a baby girl they named Mary Catherine who only lived for two days due to a serious heart condition. Both of my parents were very sad for quite a while. Their joy returned again with another pregnancy and delivery of a son they named John who struggled with asthma and lactose intolerance. Danny and I were excited to have a baby brother to play with and love.

A few years later—and being thoroughly disappointed that there were not children of color in my particular classes (only the middle school grades)—my dad asked me to come to his work for the day. I now had two brothers, and both were invited to play at some friends' homes. My dad said he had a surprise he knew I would like.

I always loved having special time alone with my dad and thought that *was* the surprise, going to the office he and his business partner, Mort, recently bought for an affordable price. The building and accompanying lot were situated on the corner of a main thoroughfare in the city of Milwaukee, Wisconsin. The neighborhood was comprised of mostly lower-income duplexes, a few single-family homes, and now the home of a photocopy-machine business and printing-service place they named Copy Incorporated.

As my dad and I drove up the busy main street, I saw various children of color. Boys and girls played in front of their homes: some jumping rope, others playing tag, and a few sitting on porch steps giggling and laughing. I knew this was going to be a great day!

My dad had already met a number of the children during the previous weeks when they moved in all the supplies and equipment for the business. The children were curious, and my dad was genuinely touched by their friendliness. They asked if he had a family, and he acknowledged he did and added that there were five of us. The children planted the idea about bringing his children to work someday. And today was that day. The children already knew my name from my dad foretelling. I tried to quickly learn everyone's name but was so taken with the beauty of the varying shades of brown from light to darker tones that I was actually mesmerized. Some of the children even had double names that were fun to practice in my head. My dad brought out stacks of photostatic paper from his inventory for us to share. Each page was treated with special chemicals.

This *magic* paper (what the children called it) reacted immediately from the rays of the sun. We all created various scenes by placing little pebbles from the sidewalk, alongside a little twig, adding a button, or paperclip, and even a pen, eraser, or pencil to design our own masterpieces. As the beams from the sun shone on the paper, the area underneath each object remained white while the surrounding area became darker. Creative spaces and shapes appeared when the objects were removed. Then, each artist printed their name (sometimes with help from a friend). The finished products were placed in the shade of the building, aka the art gallery, so that the sun would not fade the designs. We did this for hours at our sidewalk desks, creating a magnificent gallery. We laughed together as we talked and shared about our favorite colors, foods, and animals.

That afternoon when it was time for Copy Incorporated to close, it was hard to say goodbye to all my new friends who took their autographed artwork and some of mine home with them to show their family and friends. I also took my souvenirs home to cherish and preserve. On the way home, I tried to remember everything that happened during that glorious day and could not stop thanking my dad as we drove home the first few miles while I was awake. When I woke up again in our driveway, I was afraid I dreamt what happened until I gazed down at the treasures upon my lap. On top, I saw a rectangular-sized paper with flower petals in a design with two paper clips all outlined on a paper beautifully created by Sadie Jo.

I would never throw it away.

2

MERITED

My dad was the kindest man I ever met. Seeing him so generous to others made me want to be exactly like him when I grew up. Being with him always made me feel loved and safe. He always tried to be happy and interested in what my two brothers and I were involved in, which was limited to Scouts and the Crusaders Drum and Bugle Corps. He willingly accepted both parental roles of dad and mom when we were all under the age of eleven.

Our previously active mom had an undiagnosed disease for years that kept her bedridden at times and in and out of hospitals. In addition, her short-term memory was affected, which made our lives as children challenged. Finally, after ten years of many varied symptoms, she was diagnosed accurately with multiple sclerosis (MS). Not much was known about MS since information was limited and medications nonexistent. When my mom's doctors finally identified her MS diagnosis, and my parents connected with a local chapter of the National MS Society, my mom regained her vibrant personality. She was able to use her wheelchair to get around in our home and in public, too, with my dad as her inseparable date and driver. Once again, they were able to live life as a team, although at a new normal.

Late at night whenever I got up for a drink of water, I looked in my parent's room and saw my dad kneeling on the floor, leaning against the bed praying. It was a posture he maintained throughout his life until his death. His actions of surrender and trust in God impacted me greatly as a young girl. Watching him in this position of humility, I would think that's another reason why I want to be just like him when I grow up.

In the mid-1960s, racial unrest due to housing discrimination had exploded in several higher populated cities in the United States, including Milwaukee, Wisconsin. On July 30, 1967, when temperatures and tempers accelerated, a city-wide day and night curfew was declared indefinitely in Milwaukee. This was enforced through the presence of the National Guard. Their role was to help fight numerous fires that were randomly started and protect all citizens with whatever force was necessary.

It seemed surreal to see large military vehicles patrolling every neighborhood. Armed uniformed soldiers were visible from inside their vehicles as they drove up and down the empty main streets ever so slowly. Mail delivery was suspended. Nevertheless, newspaper and milk deliveries continued. Police officers accompanied the young Milwaukee Journal and Sentinel carriers and stood post near trucks laden with milk and dairy products for distribution in every neighborhood. It was a very somber time as friendly waves from citizens were not often returned. Instead, responses of cold stares and stiff postures of readied snipers made everyone uncomfortable and anxious.

During this time, my dad owned a number of tenant-occupied apartment buildings and duplexes in the inner city. Only residents in each area were allowed to be on their street per police order. This meant my dad could not freely drive on the streets in the inner city to personally check on the welfare of his tenant families. Face-to-face visits were always the best way for him to communicate. The majority of his tenants couldn't afford to have a home phone line of their own. They always appreciated when he popped in, and I tagged along whenever I was available to accompany him. He made certain that each apartment was freshly painted with colors specifically chosen by the tenants before they got settled. My dad always responded to each request by fixing anything broken and often replaced window and door screens since holes were accidentally made by the children. Meticulous notes on little pieces of scrap paper were tucked safely in his worn brown wallet with detailed information of children's names, new births, illnesses, death, and more as he genuinely cared for and about each person.

There was something else my dad did at each of his properties. He observed which of his tenants, an individual male or female or a couple, might emerge as a manager or natural-born leader at the property. He gave them more areas of responsibility and began to mentor them. Without the tenant's knowledge, he would set their rent payments aside into a separate account. Then, after a year or two, he would have a heart-to-heart talk regarding their future goals and plans. He would then ask, "Have you ever thought about owning a building like this one?" In 100% of the conversations, the tenant would respond affirmatively with a definite *yes*, which my dad already knew would be their answer. Then, they would give reasons why it would never happen to them since a bank would never lend a large amount of money without a solid credit history. My dad would smile and then bring out his handwritten record of their twelve to twenty-four monthly payments. Next, he would talk about what the concept of rent-to-own meant and how it could be implemented if they wanted to become a landlord or landlady. He would go to the local loan officer with the tenant, encourage they open their own bank account, and then present the monies he had saved for them, which was used for their loan down payment. Eventually, every one of my dad's properties was turned over to one of his tenants that lived there without any money being asked of the tenant. The buildings, apartments, or duplexes were given freely as his gift to them and future generations.

Another memory I recalled involved family participation. Once a month for years, my dad would go to a huge dark warehouse near the train station called Railroad Salvage. He always invited my two younger brothers and me to be a part of the adventure. Cases and cases of unmarked cans (mystery meals, as we referred to them) were lined row after row and stacked three-to four-feet high. In these cans were perhaps fruits, vegetables, or a canned meat or pasta product. It was anyone's guess, so selecting was dependent upon shaking sounds, weight, and size. All cases were available at deeply discounted prices. Dented cans were also available with distorted labels. Some of these slowly leaked some type of liquid, and some bulged precariously as though waiting to hatch. We usually steered clear of that section.

Every once in a while, though, my dad couldn't resist, and I would see a few oddities nestled in our home cupboard. On many occasions after shopping at the Salvage, he would set aside assorted canned products for his tenants. We would open a sample can and then match the case lot numbers and mark the other cans appropriately to let all future consumers in our family or the tenants know what was inside. When a lima or yellow bean selection occurred by mistake, it took a long time for them to be eaten. That warm July day at the end of the month would have been a normal time to bring food over to the tenants, but suddenly, life in Milwaukee seemed like a war zone.

Widespread arson of inner-city properties—both residential homes and businesses—escalated that day. After small fires began and mushroomed, evacuations occurred; uncontrolled looting followed. It saddened me to think this much hatred and destruction could be happening. Adults behaved as rebellious children, and children were frightened to see a world unravel around them.

Everyone was fixated on local and national TV and radio stations to find out what was happening. Nonstop news made Milwaukee and the other 159 cities in turmoil in the nation appear as communities of deep division. Neighborhoods were in desperate need of unity, compassion, forgiveness, and mercy. As our family watched and listened, my dad's main concerns were for the safety of our family and every one of his tenants—men, women, children, and babies of all ages.

Days later, as numerous fires left nothing but destruction and ashes, and smoldering embers sent smoke plumes vertically and horizontally, my dad and I drove to every one of his properties. All mercifully stood untouched and intact because of two words that were prominently spray painted on the sides of each: **SOUL BROTHER.**

3

MISREPRESENTED

As high school resumed in the Fall of '67, racial tensions still simmered in the City of Milwaukee. The desire to actively become involved in racial equality matters and other social issues grew steadily in my heart. I knew there was a local priest making national news because of his peaceful daytime and evening housing marches.

He was Italian in heritage and a member of the Jesuit order of priests. He connected effectively with a highly educated and extremely motivated black woman who also abhorred the discriminatory housing practices in Milwaukee. The two of them, Father James Groppi and Vel Phillips, stirred the compassion welling within my heart to become involved in an activity—one that might positively affect the living conditions of black children, their parents, and families. I shared some thoughts with my best friend, Sue, regarding what we could do to foster housing equality, especially during the daylight hours. When she heard and understood what our role could potentially be, she was fully on board. I approached my dad, the school principal, and my social studies teacher with a spirited plan proposing that if each week instead of attending one social studies class, study hall (where I socialized vs studying), and lunch period, Sue and I could participate as walkers in a peaceful housing march. All three adults agreed to this plan and felt it would be a positive way for the two of us sophomores to express social mercy and human concern as representatives of Mercy High School.

Early on, Sue and I had some hurdles of our own to conquer. The first few times we came to march with the others, they spurned us. After all, we were two white girls wearing our official school navy blue uniform jumpers just oozing with naivety. Every marcher in attendance was supposed to become part of a large circle and hold hands as a visible gesture of unity.

The organizer of the day and also Father Groppi would explain the course we would be walking along. Warnings and cautions were also emphatically given: Do not become involved in heated arguments, stone throwing, or threatening gestures. No riffraff nor disorderly conduct would be tolerated by the organizers or police guards assigned at major intersections.

Various phrases would be shared by megaphone as rallying calls, including, "Say it loud, (*clap, clap*) I'm Black, and I'm Proud (*clap, clap*)" were rehearsed. These phrases would be spoken aloud or chanted in unison throughout the walk. In conclusion at the morning instructional gathering, we would sing "We Shall Overcome" as a group before lining up along the sidewalks. Interestingly, Sue and I would be standing in the circle awkwardly holding hands with one another and rejected by the other brothers and sisters. This went on for a few weeks. We even ditched our uniforms for the morning hours and wore clothing that didn't distract from the purpose. Once the group realized we were committed, genuinely cared, and desired fair housing as much as they did, we were welcomed with hugs or crazy unique handshakes comprised of motions, movements, and fist bumps. Eventually, they included us in the opening circle with hands genuinely held together. They referred to us as *Our Mercy Girls*.

For me, Mercy High School, an all-girl private school taught by nuns of all ages, was about the most perfect school to attend for four years. At the graduation ceremony, I actually received a perfect-attendance award for never missing even one day of school during all four years. In fairness, however, I openly acknowledge that I should have simultaneously received the every-day-tardy award for obvious reasons. About six months before graduation, realizing I didn't want to leave the Mercy community, I made the necessary steps assuring I would not end that chapter of my life.

It was within those walls of the immense three-story building that I still remember the echoing effect in the hallways and especially around the marble stairwells. Even the slightest footstep, silly giggle, or stray whispered word reverberated to every ear that was listening. The grassy lot and stately building were situated prominently on the corner of 29th and Mitchell Streets, occupying two city blocks. It housed all the classrooms, a gym, an auditorium, cafeteria, library, chapel, elevator, and even a convent. This school was a place where I could step into my persona as a carefree jokester, social butterfly, and friend to all. Mercy High School was where I could be normal for a few hours during the week and forget about my mom's daily medical challenges and the many unfinished home responsibilities I had assumed since around ten years of age.

Some of the nuns who taught us throughout the four years became like older sisters. It was not uncommon for some of the younger nuns to socialize among the students after school hours and even on the weekends. One particular nun and I hit it off very well concerning social involvement opportunities. Both of us had a passion to make mercy and compassion a reality for others. One unforgettable adventure we shared was being part of Milwaukee's first annual Hunger Hike. This was a slow-paced walking activity for all ages that began and ended at the baseball stadium and meandered throughout Milwaukee for thirty miles to raise funds to feed the hungry, particularly children. The objective was to obtain sponsors committing cents or even dollars per mile walked.

During that walk, our feet became blistered and bleeding in the inexpensive canvas tennis shoes constructed without any arch support or structure that we hastily purchased. Throughout those first few miles, rich conversation between us centered upon future life decisions I needed to nail down soon. Sister MJ thoughtfully answered my numerous questions regarding her personal decision to become a nun and her satisfaction in her choices as well as her struggles. She outlined the timeline of the application process to become a Sister of Mercy and highlighted the flexibility factor to simultaneously obtain a Bachelor's degree in the field of social work, which I felt matched my natural abilities. At this juncture in life, I was truly torn with decision-making choices. A part of me wanted to have a closer relationship with God while another part of my heart wanted to serve people who were disadvantaged. An enjoyment to write from my heart also surfaced at times, and a desire to be compassionate like my dad occupied the remainder of my being. I was confused and feared I'd make a regrettable decision. Bouncing off the plethora of options milling about in my mind, I felt safe with Sister MJ. While we traveled block after block, we laughed, cried, and commiserated about the challenging walk we shared together. Understandably, she bailed on me at the twenty-mile marker as she could no longer take one more step. She handed me all her sponsorship paperwork asking if I could finish for both of us. I promised her I would.

Commitment was a value I highly treasured. I didn't question whether I would complete the walk or not. However, it would be well after the sun set, crowds thinned, and night had fallen. After I finished, I mustered my remaining strength to drive home and go right to bed. Trying to walk after waking up the next day was another story. I justified the pain and bandaged the blisters, knowing the large amount of money Sister MJ and I raised collectively for food products would temporarily satisfy the hungry bellies of children right in Milwaukee. As the pain continued over a few days, a mentality of *martyr syndrome* clouded my original pure motivation. This see-saw of good works being equivalent to personal worth affected my thinking and behavior and became an internal struggle in my life for many years. Although regrettably, I was not aware.

Weeks after the hike, I decided to begin the application process to enter the convent to become a Sister of Mercy. Two entertainment factors may have slightly influenced that decision. Sally Fields was a delightful young actress in a popular TV series that began in 1966 called *The Flying Nun* that I watched diligently every week for three years during my high school days. The main character, Sister Bertrille, resided at a convent in Puerto Rico and was able to fly when whipping winds filled her unique veil. She was always helping people in need or distress and got into many zany predicaments. I strongly identified with many of the episodes because I could close my eyes and insert myself into her life. In addition, a movie came out in 1966 with a young actress my age named Hayley Mills—*The Trouble with Angels*. It was about two girls who attended an all-girl Catholic boarding school. They constantly pulled pranks and got into mischief. Hayley decided in her senior year to stay at the convent and become a nun much to her friend's surprise and also disappointment. Perhaps some subliminal scenes in both productions took root without my knowledge.

I also applied simultaneously to the University of Wisconsin-Milwaukee for college in the Fall of '69 using some scholarship monies I had won as the Outstanding Volunteer of the Year award from Manpower, International. Becoming a social worker and a nun sounded so perfect for my future. I could commute and save money on housing, still work part-time, help at home, and know eventually I would be sent out as a degreed nun domestically or abroad to serve others.

My graduation ceremony seemed surreal, and I felt a little dishonest about the plans I had for my future. Hearing each girl's future plans announced by the emcee sounded so inspiring. I misrepresented myself since I could only share a half-truth of my plan about going to UW-M to become a social worker. None of my beloved classmates (except for one who was also entering the convent and submitted her paperwork) were even aware of the joint path I was embarking upon.

MERCY MOMENT OF TRUTH

The Parable of the Good Samaritan

"And behold, a lawyer stood up to put him to the test, saying, "Teacher, what shall I do to inherit eternal life?" He said to him, "What is written in the Law? How do you read it?" And he answered, "You shall love the Lord your God with all your heart and with all your soul and with all your strength and with all your mind, and your neighbor as yourself." And he said to him, "You have answered correctly; do this, and you will live."

But he, desiring to justify himself, said to Jesus, "And who is my neighbor?" Jesus replied, "A man was going down from Jerusalem to Jericho, and he fell among robbers, who stripped him and beat him and departed, leaving him half dead. Now by chance a priest was going down that road, and when he saw him he passed by on the other side. So likewise a Levite, when he came to the place and saw him, passed by on the other side. But a Samaritan, as he journeyed, came to where he was, and when he saw him, he had compassion. He went to him and bound up his wounds, pouring on oil and wine. Then he set him on his own animal and brought him to an inn and took care of him. And the next day he took out two denarii and gave them to the innkeeper, saying, 'Take care of him, and whatever more you spend, I will repay you when I come back.' Which of these three, do you think, proved to be a neighbor to the man who fell among the robbers?" He said, "The one who showed him mercy." And Jesus said to him, "You go, and do likewise."

—Luke 10:25–37 (ESV)

This familiar scripture from the book of Luke is often taken for granted. It has become the classic model used to label a person who has unselfishly given sacrificial help. Common examples that come to mind immediately are a roadside kindness extended to a stranger involved in an accident, a changed flat tire in inclement conditions, or the successful rescue of a drowning person from frigid waters without regard to their own life.

The phrase Good Samaritan, as related to the parable, was first used in 1843 in a sermon delivered by John Henry Newman. Luke is the only gospel out of four where this parable is mentioned. Luke, as both an author and a physician, stresses the medical aspects for healing that the unlikely Samaritan rendered as a first (and only) responder. Two other men, a priest and Levite, religious men by role, intentionally moved off the same side of the road to avoid becoming unclean. This road from Jerusalem to Jericho was eighteen miles long through an arid desert area a distance from food or water or community. This victim was beaten, robbed, described as half-dead, and undoubtedly hopeless at this point. He would have probably perished without the merciful intervention of another.

A Samaritan man who journeyed on the same road made the decision to see the invisible man others passed by. He investigated the magnitude of the situation and involved himself by putting his personal time on hold. He rendered invaluable first aid requiring him to get dirty. Then, the Samaritan invested his personal finances in this man's healing and restoration in a room he rented to care for him. He even requested an invoice from the innkeeper to keep track of additional expenses that accumulated in his absence until he returned.

The magnitude of mercy provided by the Samaritan in this account was unlimited. Yet notice how this narrative is specifically used by Jesus to publicly answer a lawyer's question regarding how he could inherit eternal life. In only a few short sentences that began with two questions, Jesus revealed Himself and related an understandable parable to personally connect with the inquirer. The lawyer was able to define neighbor and mercy and also receive Jesus' specific instruction to inherit eternal life that day.

Questions on The Quest

- What is your definition of mercy? Is it possible you've misdefined it? If so, how?

- Reflect upon a time when you were moved by compassion for someone else and acted on his or her behalf. Did you ever regret it?

PART TWO

MERCY MANIFESTED

4

MATCHED

In the fall after high school graduation, I had received a letter from the Sisters of Mercy that my application would be placed on hold for two years. The explanation was that for the first time in their 100+ year history, it was necessary for the order to revamp their outdated policies. I had felt rejected and uncertain of my future. Next, an attraction to join the Peace Corps lured me for a time, but I became bogged down in the paperwork. Months later as I ended my freshman year, I recognized the life path I traversed seemed to follow the course of the legendary 620 winding curves and hairpin turns of the famous Road to Hana in Maui, Hawaii. Choices of risk and resistance were made as I allowed my eyes, mind, and world to open to the culture of hippies, rebellion, free-thinking, and student strikes.

In May 1970, I was literally face down, frightened and stifling my whimpers in the midst of trash from all the overturned garbage cans that were strewn throughout the student union at the university. The previous day, striking students such as myself marched throughout the campus raising fists in defiance and showing solitude with the students of Kent State where shootings and deaths occurred earlier in the week. Since I lived at home off-campus, I was unaware there was a strict no student and no classes curfew on campus. I was also oblivious of the National Guard order to occupy the campus that day and use force if necessary.

Unknowingly, I drove my usual route and found parking availability in the underground structure by the student union. I didn't realize the only cars parked there had been abandoned in the chaos the day before. When I sprinted up the outside stairs to the union and got through the main entrance that was closed and uninviting, I walked into the eerily quiet place. I quickly realized I shouldn't be there at all. As I walked around and looked in all directions, I was saddened to see all the overturned couches, chairs, and tables; thrown food; spilled liquids; and overturned trash. This widespread destruction and silence at this moment were a sharp contrast to the usual music, laughter, and constant activity of students and teachers enjoying genuine camaraderie or hungry individuals in lines ordering food and making purchases.

In the seconds of unnatural silence that followed, I heard a boisterous countdown by a booming male voice … "Five. Four. Three. Two. One." At once, armed shield-yielding and masked National Guard soldiers entered every steel door. Without thought, I dove into a pile of trash between two upended plastic garbage cans, praying I wouldn't be hurt or tear gassed, although soft tears already began to flow. In only a few minutes, they called off the search in the union. The leader of this uniformed group evidently determined the union was empty and shouted, "Clear!" The rest of the soldiers responded with something else in unison and left as a unit. I knew God had truly spared me for whatever the reason this day—through His mercy. He even allowed the stains on my clothing and smells that clung to my hair and body to serve as His gentle tug and reminder that I needed to return to Him.

I was definitely confused. I didn't know who I was becoming and longed for the closeness with my dad that we had always enjoyed. My rejection by the nuns I surmised was a disappointment to my father but didn't bother sharing my presumptive thoughts. Instead, I waited until I was well into experimenting with marijuana and told my dad I was trying it once in a while with a guy I was dating he'd met numerous times and liked. Instead of my dad being angry with me and forbidding me to use marijuana or see the guy anymore, he wisely, lovingly, mercifully stated, "Linda, I'm so glad you thought enough of me to tell me yourself instead of me having to hear this from someone else. Thank you, honey."

Oh, my goodness! I turned away and ran to my bedroom where I cried and cried. Why did he give me that answer and treat me with such respect, value, and love? I wouldn't understand for many years until I became a parent and received the eternal gift of mercy. What I did know from that day forward was I would never need to use marijuana with that guy ever again, and I didn't.

It took three semesters in college of letting the words *academic warning* on my final grade report sink in. That motivated me to become a better student and instilled in me a desire to do my personal best to become a social worker. This meant letting go of certain negative relationships and reconfiguring my income sources. Evaluating the inefficiency of working four part-time jobs and learning how to study was a positive decision toward goal-achieving I was unfamiliar with before. I discovered letting go of two jobs and investing time in studying, researching, and planning projects resulted in beneficial outcomes, including grades. Discovering the value of free time was also a good choice to make.

In Wisconsin, there was an unlikely location that would be a place to meet your lifetime partner, but that was what happened on Friday, October 23, 1970. I drove three of my girlfriends forty miles north of the city to a place where bands played music and beer was served to teens who were eighteen and older. It was called Marty Zivko's Ballroom in Hartford or Zivko's for short. Personally, I didn't drink beer or alcohol products, because the few times I tried, I blacked out or acted too silly after only a few sips. I did enjoy dancing, listening to music, and especially people watching. That Friday night, the band began to play a request for a song called "The Mexican Hat Dance," which was unusual at a teen bar venue. (I've included a link in my notes to a YouTube rendition to make this more understandable to readers or listeners unfamiliar.)

A little research for this book helped me discover this beloved dance of Mexico has another traditional name of Jarabe Tapatio. It actually was a courtship dance that originated in Guadalajara, Jalisco, in the late 1800s by a man named Jesus Gonzales Rubio, a professor of music. At Zivko's, instead of dancing around a Mexican hat, I placed a discarded beer bottle I saw lying on a table onto the floor and proceeded to dance around it during the music with my girlfriend, Sue. I had part of my long blonde hair tied in back with a thin brown leather piece that bounced freely to the rhythm of this dance.

Both Sue and I evidently caught the eye and interest of two young men standing along the circumference of the dance floor leaning against the long wooden bar unsure why someone requested that traditional cultural selection. Yet they took the opportunity to check out the young women on the dance floor who actually knew how to dance to that particular song. Of course, Sue and I knew how to dance to it. We learned that dance at Mercy High School in our physical education classes along with square dancing and the polka too.

One very smiley young-faced guy cut in with his friend once that song ended and a new familiar one started. Both guys began to impress the two of us girls with their stylized footwork and smooth arm gestures choreographed perfectly to every beat of the music. Instead of leaving right after that song, both stayed to dance one more. My dance partner asked my name—and I told him—and then quickly said, "I'm Mike" and immediately got right back to dancing. His youthful appearance had me wondering if someone snuck him in with them. His coordination on the floor was very impressive, and his boyish smile and clean-cut hair was a nice change from all the hippies in college. He wore a sweater vest in fall colors and so was I, which I mentally noted as a plus. We smiled, thanked them, and parted. Then, of course, Sue and I had to speed walk to the bathroom where all good private discussions between girlfriends took place after dance encounters. We decided that both of those guys seemed nice and were definitely great dancers.

About a half-hour later, Mike came by and asked a very unexpected question. Although unique to me, it almost sounded rehearsed. He asked if he could have the leather hair strip from my hair and then give it back to me next week on a date. What? Is this a date request or a hair tie request or both? I was mulling over the aspects and consequences of the question before I answered. Then, he charmingly asked for my phone number, and he wrote it on the bottom of his shoe since he didn't have any paper available—only a pen.

I thought to myself that this was another unique approach and gave him our home phone number. He then hopped on one foot every time we made eye contact the rest of that evening so as not to look like he wanted to erase the phone number. He remembers transferring it to a piece of paper but did the hopping thing the remainder of the night for extra points.

During the week, Mike called and asked me to a movie, which I agreed to since it was to be a double date. Everything about that first date was so awful and awkward. Ironically, I had won a $100 cash prize on a radio call-in contest earlier that day, so I was excited and happy prior to the 7:00 p.m. pick-up. My mom sitting in a wheelchair and my younger brother answering the door while eating a liver sausage sandwich in his pajamas had Mike reconsidering this date for a moment or two.

When he arrived, it had started to rain, and Mike ran ahead to the car while I walked alone to the car in the drizzle and opened my own car door to the unexpected sight of two people embracing and kissing passionately in the back seat. Mike tried to make some flimsy introductions among us, but I knew facing forward would be a better idea. As Mike turned on the wipers and defroster, he warned me that some small glass pieces may fly out since he and his friend had been involved in an accident with a mailbox and had to have the windshield replaced earlier that week. Sure enough, little chards would land on my face or clothing or in my hair every once in a while.

We drove for quite a few miles, so I asked what theater we were going to and discovered we were heading to a drive-in movie to see *Night of the Living Dead*. I had never gone to a drive-in movie alone with a guy; I had only gone with my family, relatives, or girlfriends. Certainly not with three strangers in the rain. And this sounded like a horror movie which I never ever saw. Could this get any worse? Yes, since my bladder was ready to burst from the water and soft drinks I consumed prior to this nightmare. I had sole-less moccasin shoes on I didn't want to ruin in the mud puddles that surrounded the car with steamed-up windows from the backseat couple. I had pretended to fall asleep since I couldn't stand looking at the gory movie.

I told Mike I really needed to use the restroom but didn't want to ruin my shoes. Another minute would be too long, and I was ready for him to suggest I go barefoot, but instead, he surprised me and offered to carry me over his shoulder. At that point, I accepted his offer. We sat in the concession stand for the remainder of the movie, staying dry, warm, and awake, eating sugary snack foods and talking. He seemed like a really nice guy after getting to know him better. I discovered we had opposite personality traits—he had a poor relationship with his dad since his mother's death when he was only fourteen, and he hadn't been to church in a very long time. He wondered about my mother's condition and if it was hereditary, why I was going to school to become a social worker, what I didn't like about the movie, and how I won $100 earlier in the day. Time must have passed by quickly because the theater manager let us know the movie ended, and he was closing up the food area to clean up.

At the end of this unconventional date, we dropped off the two back seat occupants at the location where their car was parked. As we drove a few more blocks to my home, Mike made some small talk. It seemed as though he was a little nervous. In front of my house, he turned off the car and shifted to park. He was hoping I'd kiss him and tried leaning in. That was definitely not my plan, so I opened my door for a quick exit but thanked him for staying in the concession stand area with me to avoid the scary movie and especially for sharing parts of his life. We both weren't totally sure there would be a second date since there was little we had in common.

5

MITIGATED

Neither Mike nor I could remember when or where our second date took place. We do know something drew us to take a second date together without Mike's friends along. Infatuation led to falling in love, getting engaged, and willing to wait for our wedding day and honeymoon one month after college graduation.

As our love for each other deepened exponentially, a number of things in our life also happened. Mike had been drafted with number thirteen because of a nationally enforced military lottery that selected his birthdate of February 22nd. Miraculously, however, he was not sent overseas for active duty. Mike's co-worker explained the predicament of being drafted within months to his father who served as a high-ranking official in the National Guard. This man explained other options to Mike that included signing up for the National Guard right away. Mike talked over all the choices with me, decided the National Guard option to be the best, and left for basic training. I was a student at UW-Milwaukee and also working a number of jobs. When he left, I could remain focused on school, and he could satisfy the requirements of the draft. Since we already had our wedding date of June 23, 1973, picked out two years in advance, we knew this plan was wise and would work for our future.

Mike was extremely good at playing baseball and was randomly asked during basic training to play on the Army team as the first baseman, which assured us he would remain stateside. He agreed and enjoyed this role during his duration there. Throughout his time away, he wrote me love letters complete with little pictures he drew before bedtime and lights out (usually from a bathroom stall). His letters arrived almost every day, which I still have saved and tied together with a ribbon.

As a National Guardsman, Mike returned to civilian life after a short period of time in comparison to those sent off to serve in Vietnam. Approximately seven months before our wedding, Mike and I were invited by a friend of my brother named Gary to an evening that would impact us for eternity. A well-known doctor packed a room as he shared some interesting things about Jesus and the Bible.

Mike and I were quite involved as a couple in various groups and projects in the Catholic Church I had grown up in and loved attending. We thought it made great sense to have a date there since Gary had kept asking us to go for at least two months. As we arrived at the entrance, the people seemed genuinely nice and friendly. Gary saw us come in and immediately brought us over to a table where books and pamphlets were being given and sold. He wanted us to meet a man named John, then introduced us to him.

After a few pleasantries were exchanged among us, John invited Mike and me out for coffee the following week at a restaurant nearby. We were too shy and embarrassed to tell him that we never drank coffee before. Instead, we agreed to the time and place John suggested. Then, we went into the crowded room and found two open seats. The talk that night captivated me as this practicing ER physician named Mark read some Bible verses and related them to all present in such a personal way. He talked about Jesus as his friend and shared some stories about patients he treated in the ER. As he concluded, he prayed for everyone there. I truly didn't want that evening to end. He invited everyone back for the following Wednesday, and I squeezed Mike's hand signaling I would like to return if he felt the same way I did.

On Friday at 6:00 p.m., John and another man met us at the Big Boy restaurant where he invited us. John ordered a pot of coffee for the four of us and asked if we needed cream or sugar. We both said yes and were handed the metal creamer and a large cylindrical glass sugar dispenser with a cute metal flap to pour away. Then, we loaded up our cups to dilute the taste of the coffee using the spoons to turn the black liquid into a light brown sweetened beverage.

John brought out two pieces of blank paper—one for each of us from a folder he carried. He said this was going to be a psychological test. In my mind, I thought I would do well on this since test taking in college was second nature for me. He asked Mike and I to make a tic-tac-toe image large enough to fit on the whole paper. Then, he asked us to draw an answer to the nine questions he asked using one square of the outline per answer. This took several minutes. Then, the waitress came back to replace the coffee pot we had already emptied into our four cups plus refills for John and his friend. Both Mike and I tried to do our best while John patiently waited for us to put the finishing touches on each square. John studied both of our papers, then proceeded to ask me one intrusive question followed by another that seemed as though it did not relate to our purpose of this coffee date. He asked me, "If you die tonight, do you know where you would spend eternity?" This kind of surprised me, and I quickly responded with "heaven." Then, he asked, "Why?"

I told this inquisitive stranger how I had taken care of my mom since I was ten, taught a children's religious class called CCD for years, and went on and on about all the good works I had performed that would obviously be rewarded. In harsh reply, John didn't mince words and shared how wrong I was in my thinking and that I'd be going to hell instead. He used terms that were graphic and to the point to let me know my good works were comparable to filthy rags. I felt as though I stood face to face with truth and said in desperation, "What can I do then to get to heaven?" He said, "Absolutely nothing." Then, he went on to share how Jesus had done everything for me, but I needed to acknowledge I was a sinner. I stopped to think about sin in a new way for the very first time.

Up until that moment, I had only thought of sin in terms of a checklist that I was able to erase with an apologetic prayer, positive action, or social service activity. Although I considered myself to be religious and self-righteous all my life, something happened in that moment for the first time. I actually realized the effect my personal sins had in crucifying Jesus. John asked if I wanted to truly repent of my sins, and I nodded my head.

He had asked me to pray aloud in our booth, and I really didn't care who was in that restaurant or what anyone thought. I really was so thankful that this conversation made complete sense, and stirred my soul. Inside, I felt so happy and truly joy-filled. This evening lingered on for many more hours, however, as John and Mike got into all kinds of discussions that I tuned out. I had some intestinal issues from the many cups of caffeinated coffee I drank to be polite and was frequenting the women's bathroom that all three men were oblivious to.

When I got home that night, I took a gift from my dresser I had received two days before and held it close to my heart, smiling and chuckling. It was a Christmas present from a co-worker named Pat. She had given me this pocket-sized black Bible of the New Testament, Psalms, and Proverbs with gold-edged pages and my name engraved in gold on the front. Two days before, I thought it was a foolish present to receive, but that night, I cherished the gift, the Word of God that John had encouraged me to begin reading daily. What timing—I already had my own personalized mini Bible. I opened the cover, and familiar verses and passages seemed brand new.

Just as changes occur ever so slightly to a seed that is planted and germinates in fertile ground, the new life of Christ in me began to grow. I became more aware and sensitive to the fact that I had been mitigating sin in my life. It seemed that when I would begin to think that I had dealt with a particular sin in my life, including a critical spirit, unwillingness to forgive, or jealous thoughts, God would gently remind me of the next area we needed to work on together.

Then, one day, a situation I was involved in almost two years before came flooding back with fury, causing me to weep uncontrollably as I recognized for the first time I partook in the loss of another person's life and future.

During one late afternoon in 1971, I sat in my little one-person drive-up photo booth. I was working on my homework for a social studies class when a car drove alongside. Customers would drop off rolls of camera film at my little place called The Photo Hut. The film would be sent out for developing and returned in forty-eight hours. I loved this job because I could interact with all the customers who would often encourage me to look at their photos with them and listen as they told accompanying stories.

That day, the driver's window rolled down, and a friend from the past choked out words in the midst of his tears. This was a man a few years younger than me whom I had mentored in the Youthpower, Inc. summer job program. He always had a smile. I had watched him gain a sense of direction in life and make strides toward becoming an adult over a three-year period. At that moment, he stumbled over his words, saying he needed to borrow $100 dollars as soon as possible. To put this dollar amount in perspective, I made $1.65 an hour, and $100 was half of my tuition in college for a semester that I paid myself. Yet I was already willing to listen to the why.

David began to share he had been dating a young woman for about ten weeks and had felt he'd fallen in love with her. She divulged to him that in her previous relationship that had become abusive, she had no idea she'd become pregnant through force. David stated after her pregnancy had been confirmed the day before, she threatened to kill herself. He stayed awake at her home the whole night watching her so she wouldn't take her life. If she had taken her life, David told me he would have to take his life also.

They researched only one option. It was for the total cost of an abortion in New York (only legal state), plus round-trip transportation and a taxi for them. The dollar amount needed beyond their combined savings was $100. He asked if I would lend them the final amount. I was never faced with a decision of this magnitude before and asked David to leave me alone for a half-hour, and I'd have an answer. He nodded and drove off. I sat numb and stunned. What criteria could I use to make a decision? I pulled out a blank piece of copy paper and proceeded to hand draw a scale with a triangle fulcrum in-between two dishes that hung from an elongated bar across. To this day, I can remember the two standing stick figures I drew with their hands touching each other positioned on the left dish. Then, on the opposite side, I drew a small face and oval-shaped simulated blanket horizontally on the empty dish. I looked back and forth over and over again at the two dishes and began to cry, wanting to make the best choice in a merciful and compassionate way.

In this surreal moment in time, I felt I would be the sole decision-maker. Their situation became my situation. I began reasoning in my mind with my limited knowledge and vision. My decision was to value two adult lives that I would save from an early death. I withdrew the $100 from my savings account, and I gave it to David the following day. At peace with my decision, I reasoned this was best because I had saved his life and the life of his girlfriend.

Two years later after what I will refer to as my salvation experience of being fully forgiven of all past sinfulness and no more eternal separation from Jesus Christ, the memory of the $100 abortion loan came flooding back. This time, however, it was with the perspective of the total truth of that day with no opportunity for mitigating the horror of my past sin and effects. I realized my full participation and culpability.

Thou shalt not kill.

Murderer.

Regret.

Condemning words circled my mind and heart. Remorse and sorrow surrounded my soul. Instead of feeling I had saved two adult lives, I was fully aware of my role in taking an unborn baby's life by making that abortion possible through my $100 participation. I also realized my altruistic action actually prohibited God's plan to work in David and his girlfriend's lives as well. Perhaps they would have sought and trusted Him as their Savior and Redeemer in their situation.

It was in those moments that seemed like hours that I understood so personally for the first time what God's abundant mercy meant. Even now, I still cannot fathom the depth of His forgiveness and precious love for me.

6

MOTHERED

Getting married was such a joyful time to share with family and friends. It felt tropically hot on June 23, 1973, and my face actually hurt from smiling so much that day. We had to postpone our honeymoon due to the annual required two-week National Guard Camp Mike was obligated to fulfill. Our honeymoon was well worth waiting for and included staying two days and one night at a lovely hotel overlooking the breathtaking Niagara Falls on the Canadian side. For the rest of our honeymoon, we camped in a new *non-waterproof* pup tent and traveled the countryside for nine days in our cozy, bright yellow Volkswagen Super Beetle. This carefree time to travel as a newlywed couple confirmed we were going to live happily ever after, only the two of us—for a few years anyway.

Being married was a time of some adjustments. Even though we had dated for two and a half years, we had never lived together until we were married. Some little and a few major areas needed to be worked through and discussed with mutual agreement and understanding. After our planned five-year wait, we could begin our family of twelve children, which Mike thought would be the perfect number.

* * *

BIRTH ANNOUNCEMENT #1

However, in only eleven months, Kim, our first child, was born. I truly enjoyed the pregnancy, that is, once the daily morning sickness subsided well into the second trimester. I was uncertain how to be a mom, but I was willing to learn. Someone had given me a lovely book titled *Meditations for the Expectant Mother*. It actually addressed many topics I had not even considered. The prayers at the end of the meditations were ones I read and prayed again and again, always sensing God's peace and joy afterward.

The timing of Kim's birth on May 11, 1974, was one day before Mother's Day that year. The day after she was born, a lovely pink carnation cradled by baby's breath and greenery was strategically positioned on my hospital breakfast tray. A small card that read, "Happy Mother's Day" was attached to a pink ribbon wrapped around the neck of the narrow vase. It was surreal to be wished a Happy Mother's Day by the staff and so many strangers in the hospital. However, parts of my body confirmed the reality of the title when trying to walk to the bathroom or in the hall to the nursery.

Mike smirked a little at first but also enjoyed his new title of Dad by hospital staff and welcomed the step-by-step lessons from the friendly nurse in the proper way to hold and support the head and neck of Baby Kim all bundled like a burrito in a perfectly wrapped blanket. Whether Kim was a boy or a girl, the name we both agreed on was our only choice. In fact, all of our future eleven children would be given first names that could be interchanged as male or female and began with the letter *K*, or so we thought. That was the original plan.

That year, Mike's required two-week National Guard Camp was moved from the end of June to mid-May, which meant he had to pack his belongings and leave his five-day-old daughter and me at home to bond and adjust. She already knew my voice and turned toward me when I spoke or attempted to sing. During our first week together, I played a cassette of soothing lullabies every evening. In those first few days, I prayed for our little family to be used by God wherever He would lead us as His ambassadors. This became the focus of my prayers that would continue through many decades of our life.

* * *

BIRTH ANNOUNCEMENT #2

After a year and half, we moved to a nearby suburb of Milwaukee when I was pregnant with our second child. This home was a new construction that we had the opportunity to work on since the builder was my dad's best friend. Mike was very skilled with tools and knowledgeable about construction, so we saved a lot of money doing things that we could as we had the funds to do so. Wallpapering, mudding walls, framing, landscaping, heating, air-conditioning, gutters, and painting were some of the projects that could be tackled individually by Mike or both of us as a team.

After we had some large projects out of the way, I provided childcare in our home daily for two families' children. The working moms in that subdivision noticed

I didn't work outside the home, loved playing with Kim, and was neighborly to all, so they asked me if I would be interested in caring for their children. I wasn't sure other people's children would find me to be nurturing and a fun mom but offered to give it a try.

I enjoyed getting to know and love every child or baby sent our way. God faithfully equipped me to be a pseudo-mom to each precious child he brought, even one who would return to our lives almost twenty years later.

Deep friendships were forged, memories made, and great times shared. Everyone anxiously anticipated the birth of our next child due before Thanksgiving who we would name Kary. Labor began, so we headed to the hospital on November 22, 1976. Then, after an unsuccessful all-nighter of walking the halls, laying on this side and then the opposite side to promote more productive contractions, we were discharged and sent home.

We also anticipated the birth of a family business at the same time. It was a Christian book and gift store we named *The Apple of His Eye*. We had all the shelves stocked, displays and counters readied throughout the store, and received an occupancy permit from the city of West Allis for this transformed bakery location. The OPEN sign was not in place as we delayed opening and operating until after Baby Kary's birth. We even had set up a little nursery and play area for our children with an available kitchenette in a bright room cordoned off in the store. We thought it would be ideal for all four of us to live life together as a family in the store whenever I could come for a visit with the kids.

Since Baby Kary's due date had come and gone, Mike decided we should open the store on November 27th with a grand opening that coincided with Black Friday. So much of our business loan was tied up in stock and inventory that needed to be sold. It was a very profitable Friday and Saturday, as so many friends, family, and even real customers welcomed our new ministry. Everyone was so encouraging. I was physically uncomfortable and not sleeping well either. After church on Sunday and playing with Kim all afternoon, I decided against returning to the store until after Kary's birth.

On December 5th while eating lots of goodies and socializing at a Christmas Cookie exchange, the event grew extra exciting. Dear friends from Mercy High School hosted this special gathering. My friend, Mary, sat next to me and asked, "What do contractions feel like?" Her question caught me off guard. I had been eyeing up the varieties of cookies spread over the kitchen counters that I would be taking home in exchange for the Hershey Kiss cookies I brought to share.

After refocusing, I noticed my contractions had grown stronger throughout the day. I was used to ignoring them the past few days, not wanting to repeat the false labor scenario anytime soon. Mary boldly asked if she could place her hand on my belly for the next few minutes, and I reluctantly agreed. She then giggled. "How do you know when it's time to go to the hospital?" I calmly explained, "When the contractions are less than five minutes apart."

She slipped her watch off her wrist, tightly gripping the face with one hand while pressing her other hand against my pregnant belly. Mary's awkward position drew unwanted attention to our side of the room as everyone seemed to hold their breath. Since the next contraction was three and a half minutes later, Mary stood up and took charge. She turned into a drill sergeant and announced that no one was permitted to let me drive home in my own car. Then, she grabbed my purse and vigorously dug through it like a dog burying a bone. She grasped my wad of car keys and ran to the front door as I came after her to retrieve them.

I suddenly knew my relaxing afternoon visiting with friends and enjoying cookies had come to an abrupt halt. As I tried to convince her I was absolutely fine to drive back home in time for Baby Kary to be delivered safely, my reassurance fell on deaf ears. Instead, she tossed my keys into the middle of a snowbank and assigned Kathy to escort me in her heated van complete with a Citizen's Band (CB) radio. Kathy turned on her radio, mic in hand, gave her handle name, and alerted anyone listening that there was a woman in labor ready to deliver a child any minute en route to meet her husband.

Hospital names and locations were shouted one by one from helpful listeners amid static-crackling sounds. My two plenteous plates of mounded cookies covered with foil slid this way and that across the front van floor after each exaggerated turn and curve. I felt completely calm, but Kathy did not. I stifled my laughs while looking out the window wondering when this would end. I opened the window ever so slightly as I became overheated and light-headed. And then, it started first as a trickle followed by a stream. Dark decadent chocolate from various cookies melted in the eighty-plus-degree temps from the heat blowing forcefully through the floor vents. My shoes were in the midst of the rivulets that swirled and circulated.

As Kathy pulled into our driveway, her rhythmic horn blasts announced our arrival and caught Mike's attention. I was so glad to see both Mike and Kim smiling at our front door. Mike looked confused as to why I came home so early without our car. I thanked Kathy for the safe arrival and handed Mike the two messy plates of cookies he was looking forward to eating with a glass of milk. He saw my shoes covered with chocolate and caramel patterns that I removed for thorough cleaning at a later date. We all laughed and laughed.

He asked if I felt ready to meet Baby Kary. I assured him he would need to put the closed sign out at our store for the Monday morning customers. It read, "Having A Baby, Closed Today." My brother, John, and his fiancé, Nancy, came over to stay with Kim while we took the sign to the store and then checked into the OB department to have our second baby.

At 1:02 a.m. on December 6, 1976, our eight-pound-two-ounce son, Kary, was delivered after some very strong contractions and hard pushes. He was an early Christmas gift to our family born on the feast day of St. Nicholas. This Saint was a young man known and beloved as a magnanimous gift-giver to the poor, children, and so many throughout Turkey.

A few days later, the hospital provided a private lovely candlelight dinner in the hospital room, which was such a special time. Baby Kary slept soundly in his little rollable isolette parked right next to our candlelit table. We enjoyed every moment as we watched him sleep peacefully in his tiny bed so thankful for his life and the many adventures we would share together in the years to come.

In the weeks following Kary's birth, he exhibited noticeable breathing problems as he gasped for air and often sounded congested. He was diagnosed with asthma. We were advised to have a humidifier running most of the time to minimize the dry air in our home environment since he often struggled to breathe.

That meant curtailing the bookstore family visiting plan since the little room we fixed up had ceilings and walls not conducive to an ongoing humidifier. Two dear friends, Bev and Fay, volunteered their time regularly in the store to allow Mike to cover all the hours of the bookstore operation so he could leave the store at times and enjoy interacting with the two children.

* * *

BIRTH ANNOUNCEMENT #3

Our next major venture after the bookstore was the purchase of a home and 101-acre parcel about thirty miles west of where we lived. We wanted to open and operate a Christian retreat center in this unique location and didn't fully realize the magnitude of this large undertaking. After living in this new rural area for a little while, the four of us were excited to welcome baby number three. We no longer had one K-name ready, but instead, we chose a name that was more biblically inspired and gender specific.

We kept the same ob-gyn doctors, so the prenatal visits were more of a field trip with two young children to accompany me. It was on one of those trips into West Allis that Kary, who hadn't been very verbal at this point, blurted out a very lengthy first word/phrase/sentence that made us laugh and cheer. For months, he'd pointed at something and grunted, which alerted his older sister, Kim, to guess and guess until he eventually nodded because she'd guessed right. It gave Kary a way to communicate with her but limited his attempt to expand his own vocabulary.

And then, as we drove east on I-94 passing an area built up with fast food restaurants, Kary observed, "Look, over there, on the hill, McDonald's." It was his first string of words put together—not two or three but seven clearly in an understandable sentence. I almost stopped the car mid-traffic at that moment. Kim and I cheered with delight, and Kary gleefully repeated the same sentence over and over and over again. After the doctor's appointment on the way back home, we had to stop at that same McDonald's for a little ice cream sundae celebration.

The summer of 1979 heated up quickly, and living in a rural setting made it feel even hotter. This beautiful property we bought had an established asparagus garden and canes and canes of delicious juicy raspberries. I knew absolutely nothing about growing food, harvesting, or canning, but I learned quickly. My days of city living, nearby grocery stores, friends calling often, and neighbors visiting or popping in to borrow or share were becoming distant memories.

I still knew how to make friends, though, if I could find some. Since the nearest neighbor was a quarter of a mile away, I joined a group of women called the Homemakers of America. I invited them to hold all their meetings at our home for the rest of the year. It was good for me because I was unfamiliar with the rural postal numbers that didn't show up on most maps way before GPS and cell phones. In fact, this area was so rural they had their own telephone system of landlines that used only four digits.

These domesticated and talented women took me under their wings and taught me many things. I shared some Bible lessons during meetings on occasion. They even had a sweet baby shower for us after our baby was born.

As with the other two children, this little one was born after her due date. We took a family picture while I was in labor by a leafy tree in our front yard, knowing there was time before delivery. I packed up all sleepover items so the two kids could stay the night at Aunt Nancy and Uncle John's, and we could welcome our next baby into our lives. By far, this baby's delivery seemed to be going exactly like clockwork.

Baby Sarah made her debut on July 2, 1979, weighing in at seven pounds and ten ounces. Her name meant "God's Princess" and was a prophetic choice for her life. She and I bonded over the 4th of July holiday as we watched beautiful fireworks explode on two different nights visible from the expansive hospital windows of the fourth floor. As we were discharged later in the week, Mike and I marveled how tiny Sarah's hands and feet were as we placed her into a carrier for her first car ride. We were so thankful to God for His precious gift to all of us.

The other two children were so excited for Sarah to join our family and often put their own needs aside until she was fed, rocked, and diapered. They could hardly wait until we shared reading time together on the couch. During that summer, we also attempted to add a dog named Toby and a cat named Jenny without success.

Every day in the afternoon after lunchtime but before naps, the three kids, Toby, and I gathered ourselves together to get the mail. Our driveway was a quarter-mile away from the road, so coordinating the mail trip in sunny weather was a project.

Five-year-old Kim pulled two-and-a-half-year-old Kary in the wagon while I placed Baby Sarah toward me in my front carrier to stay safely snuggled. Toby ran alongside us, freely veering off in and out of the various plants on the property often covered with bits of leaves, burrs, and insects.

We made sure to stop every few feet to check out flowers, bugs, pebbles, and weeds along the blacktopped driveway there and back again. As we retrieved the mail from the big black metal box, cars with drivers and their passengers, often friends and sometimes strangers, waved and beeped as they whizzed by. It often felt like we were living out an episode from *Little House on the Prairie*.

Mike got a job at Briggs & Stratton since he was a journeyman sheet metal worker. Unfortunately, this position was a long commute at forty-eight miles away. Still, his job supported our family. In time, it became obvious that we needed to sell our home and property. The high property cost that included utilities, taxes, and insurance exceeded our income. However, during this time, God miraculously worked out our finances and provided in so many ways and situations for us that another book could be written to detail His mercy and faithfulness.

During a prayer time session at the one and only women's retreat held in our home, many of the twenty-two women prayed for God to sell our homestead that was listed for a while. That same day, our broker contacted an investor he knew and shared the details of the residence and accompanying sixteen acres. The investor felt the timing to purchase would be good for his situation and said he'd make it work. He didn't even need to look at the property and bought it without ever walking through. Many other things happened during that one retreat that allowed all present to see God in His mercy at work in so many women's lives and circumstances.

* * *

BIRTH ANNOUNCEMENT #4

We moved in February 1980 on a fairly warm winter day in Wisconsin. We rented half of a small side-by-side ranch home from my brother, John, his wife, Nancy, and their two sons. A little over a year later, both Nancy and I were pregnant and due within ten weeks of each other.

The activity in the home was constant as the children enjoyed playing with their cousins only a few feet away from each other. Some physical complications made this pregnancy difficult as sciatic pain kept me on my back several hours each day for many months.

For me, this was an extremely difficult time of constant physical pain because it limited me from being fully involved as a mother to our children. My prayer life suffered, too, as I turned inward and neglected God's Word, which would have been comforting and encouraging.

I remember a few women from the Bible study I attended asking to pray for me. Actually, my initial response was resistance. The day they prayed was when I felt the need to make a full surrender to whatever God was doing in my life that needed to be done. Tears followed in the quietness of that moment, and I felt the return of joy, restoration, and an unexplainable peace from God. Oddly, I felt ready for what would happen in the days to come.

Baby number four would be named April Joy or Jeremy John (JJ), expected on May 23, 1982. Since the other three children were all born around two weeks after their due date, I planned Kim's eighth birthday party on May 7th for her school girl friends at our home. I had purchased the birthday decorations, made her cake and food, and readied final plans. Early that morning around 5:00 a.m., my back hurt as it did everyday, but something didn't seem right, so I let Mike know. Other symptoms quickly followed, so we knocked on John and Nancy's door to let them know we were headed to the hospital. Nancy was also awake rocking her sleeping newborn son, Christopher. We asked if she could rest on our couch until our kids got up. She quickly agreed and offered to also feed them breakfast with her children.

At 7:07 a.m.—not too long after we got settled in our room—Baby Jeremy arrived more than two weeks early at six pounds and two ounces—making him the lightest child and easiest delivery. I delivered sitting down in a brand-new birthing chair the hospital staff used for the first time.

The hospital had purchased this chair as an alternative for delivering moms with severe back pain, so we all decided it was a good idea for me to be one of the first to use it. It was a great decision, and once JJ was delivered, all back pain immediately resolved. I felt like dancing and made the attempt to get out and praise God for this baby, but they told me to sit down so they could finish the rest of the birthing procedures. Both Mike and I beamed with joy and gratitude as Baby Jeremy was placed in my arms, never to leave my heart.

We called home from the hospital room to share the news with the children. Each child was so excited for various reasons that were so endearing to hear and remember. Kim said she wasn't sad that she wouldn't have a birthday party because JJ was the best gift she could ever receive. Kary was thrilled JJ was a boy so he could have his own brother instead of just next-door boy cousins. Sarah said she was so happy we had a baby she could hold whenever she wanted in our own side of the house. Mike and I were grateful for another gift from God we could love and cherish in our 900-square-foot abode.

Life continued with no back pain at all, and during the next few days after bringing Jeremy home, we rescheduled Kim's birthday party. He was the hit of her party as she beamed with joy. Jeremy's arrival into our family was a seamless transition for everyone. We all took turns holding or looking at him for hours.

Two weeks later, I became so ill with constant vomiting for a few days. This was concerning since I was nursing Jeremy. In fact, we had never bottle fed any of the children whom I had nursed until they were more than one year old. We called the doctor but were met with more confusion and delays. On the fourth day of being so weak and unable to produce any more milk, Mike took me to the ER, and Nancy fed Jeremy with some of the formula she had for Chris.

It was hard for me to say goodbye to all of the children not knowing what was wrong. An ultrasound showed there was a mass in my abdominal area, and they scheduled surgery for the following day. I was dehydrated and needed an extraordinary amount of fluids to prevent more problems. Bag after bag of fluids was administered intravenously. Water in any form—not even a few ice chips—wasn't allowed at this time. No visitors except Mike were permitted. He was clearly worried and was off work without pay to care for the children along with Nancy's help and help from his sister, Darlene.

In the hospital, some of the nurses on the floor were part of my women's Bible study. Together, we prayed for God's mercy for Mike at this time who suddenly realized twelve children would no longer be what he wanted. Even three and a newborn were more than enough.

Two weeks later, I was discharged after major surgery that resulted in removing my appendix from an enclosed sac. Days before the removal, it had burst inside the sac but remained miraculously intact. When removed, it caused peritonitis throughout my body, which had to be addressed daily with sixteen rounds of antibiotic injections.

I definitely lost baby weight during my hospital stay and had many staples and drain tubes placed in my shrinking abdomen. God sustained me daily in His mercy and through His strength and grace. He provided an elderly roommate next to me the entire time named Irma for His unique purpose.

Since she and I were both very ill, we had some heart-to-heart spiritual talks. She was open to me praying for her and watching some spiritually encouraging shows together during the long days confined to our beds. She accepted Jesus as her Lord and Savior and ultimate healer before she died two weeks after discharge. Her adult children had prayed for her to accept Christ for years and years and got to see the transformation in her. I felt God gave me her at my weakest time to watch Him work in her life. The family invited me to the funeral, which was a joyous time of celebration.

In the hospital, I continued to pump my breasts and throw out the tainted milk twice a day. I wanted to breast-feed Jeremy with safe and nutritious milk when released someday. It was difficult and tiring to do but a daily goal to attain. After my surgery, the doctor told Mike that because of the severity of the infection and weakness, we needed to prepare for the worst. The doctor also recommended that if I improved, I should refrain from a future pregnancy since my organs and abdomen had been damaged so badly during and after surgery.

Mike agreed and assured me that four children were fine unless God brought another child to our door someday. He did the best he could as a father to our four children when I was hospitalized. We both appreciated the two different and important roles we shared as parents and grew even closer than we already were. We fell behind in our bills after Mike's unpaid six-week medical leave of absence, yet God faithfully sustained us.

Six months later on December 24, 1982, we moved to our own 1200-square-foot two-story home in Waukesha. It was almost 60 degrees, which broke a record for the day! Many dear friends in town visiting with their families for the Christmas weekend made this move possible for us in only a few hours. They even helped set up our beds.

Some people we didn't know came at the same time and brought us a Christmas tree with lights and many wrapped gifts for each child and us. They put some food in our refrigerator and on the counter and only told us Merry Christmas and that Jesus loved us. Strangely, we received more Christmas presents that year than we ever had in our lives, and we didn't even know where they came from and who the people were who brought them. It was such a visible compassionate demonstration of God's mercy and love. This impacted us in an eternally focused way. These unidentified people left quickly but only after many hugs, tears, smiles, and thanks from all.

The moving boxes were placed everywhere, so trying to locate the one I had specially identified with the words *Christmas Clothing* was a definite challenge. Mike and the three older children needed to get ready in their holiday attire to attend Grandma Millie's and Grandpa Bucko's home for the annual Christmas Eve meal and gift exchange with all the cousins.

Regrettably, no one located the marked box in time for their departure. The clashing outfits on the children were unique and took the attention off the mismatched pairs of socks and even shoes on their feet. They were all so excited to go, which brought me great joy as we exchanged hugs and kisses.

Earlier that day, Baby JJ began teething for the first time. He was in dire misery as his gums swelled, and a low fever lingered. Tears gently flowed down his warm cheeks as soft moans sounded occasionally. My goal the rest of the afternoon and evening was to nurse and soothe him in this quiet, unfamiliar place that became our home a few hours earlier.

I scooted the wooden rocker over to a window so I could look out at the streetlights and surrounding sky. The six-year-old rocker had effectively calmed Kary and Sarah during times when they were not feeling well, couldn't sleep, or teethed and was going to help me be a merciful mother to JJ on this Christmas Eve night. Since it was still fairly warm outside, I left the front door open to our enclosed porch area. Across the street, I saw the neon sign of a small restaurant. I thought it read: *Jimmy's Ghetto Pizza.*

The real name was actually *Jimmy's Grotto Pizza.* I wondered what kind of a neighborhood we moved to but knew, without a doubt, God had provided this home in this location at a price we could afford. Then, I thought of Joseph and Mary. She gave birth to Baby Jesus in a place they were unfamiliar with too. I looked up in the sky, and I saw so many sparkling stars as clear as jewels. It felt almost surreal. Whenever Jeremy began to cry in pain, I sang *Silent Night* in a soft voice, and he stopped crying and nodded off to sleep for a little while. Being a mom in that quiet moment reminded me of the extraordinary privilege it is to parent. Many friends and family were unable to conceive or miscarried at various stages of pregnancy, yet this night, I held this little life close to my heart, never to take for granted.

A few months went by, and we settled into the neighborhood and unique rhythm of Waukesha's culture. The children quickly made friends in the neighborhood, and soon after, the neighborhood children gravitated to our home for playtime. I began to provide childcare for four children in the neighborhood on a regular schedule. More children were added to that number as our family embraced each child. Every child we added blended well with ours. Sharing Bible stories, lessons, games, food, recipes, and activities made each day a fun and growing time for all of us as a family.

* * *

SURPRISE ANNOUNCEMENT #5

On one chilly evening in October 1983, it was already dark by 7:30 p.m. Our four children ages one through nine were settling down and getting ready for bedtime. Two had school the following day, so lunches were being packed and uniform clothing laid out.

Our doorbell rang from outside our enclosed porch followed by a steady knock on the inside door. I opened the door and saw a young thirty-something woman in a long, tan, quilted coat clutching a toddler peering curiously from inside a loosely wrapped periwinkle blue blanket. She had a small piece of paper firmly held between her thumb and first finger that she glanced at and asked, "Are you Linda?"

I nodded and ushered her inside our living room to an upholstered chair. She began to unwrap the little boy seated on her lap who appeared to be a little older than Jeremy. He began interacting with our four children at a cautious pace. All names were exchanged, and she introduced herself as Mary and her son Richard.

Mary explained how she had been given our family name by Carlene, a mutual friend I attended a weekly women's AGLOW Bible study with for a number of years. Mary went to nursing school with Carlene in northern Wisconsin, and they had stayed in contact since Mary moved to Waukesha. This particular night, Mary had fled from a horrendous situation involving her husband. She ran for six blocks down unfamiliar streets and alleys to protect her son's life and hers to hopefully find safety in our home.

Richard and Mary became a special part of our lives that began that night in 1983 and continued daily until the summer of 1988. Her marriage was annulled, and she maintained a cute apartment for her and Richard near our home. She often worked both first and third shifts as a highly skilled nurse at the local hospital to support her and Richard.

She needed to sleep during second shift and get some necessary errands and routine house chores done, so Richard often stayed overnight, which worked out very well. Ironically, he and Mike shared the same birthdate. We fully accepted Richard as our own son because God brought him to our door, literally.

MERCY MOMENT OF TRUTH

Mary's Song—The Magnificat

And Mary said: "My soul glorifies the Lord and my spirit rejoices in God my Savior, for He has been mindful of the humble state of His servant. From now on all generations will call me blessed, for the Mighty One has done great things for me—holy is His name. His mercy extends to those who fear Him, from generation to generation. He has performed mighty deeds with His arm; He has scattered those who are proud in their inmost thoughts. He has brought down rulers from their thrones but has lifted up the humble. He has filled the hungry with good things.

—Luke 1:46-53 (ESV)

In these heartfelt verses spoken by a young woman named Mary, a picture of humble submission and full surrender to the coming Lord Jesus is beautifully revealed. She, along with previous generations of Israelites, waited expectantly in hope for a Savior. Her desire was to welcome a Redeemer whose life would be the only acceptable sacrifice for her sin and the sins of every person. Mary's response, in praise and worship, addressed God intimately as "my Savior."

How amazing it must have been to be visited by an angelic being. His direct message that she was chosen to carry the Savior as her own child did not cause her to run away in fear. Instead, she acknowledged the joy in her spirit along with the spontaneous response to glorify her Lord and Savior.

Her acceptance of her appointed role as the mother of her Savior is reflective of deep spiritual maturity and familiarity with scripture combined with the simplicity of childlike faith and obedience. God's extension of His eternal mercy as a gift to each person who fears Him from generation upon generation is as relevant for today as it was when Mary expressed her acceptance of His mercy and grace.

Young Mary's lowly status in the community as an unschooled teen had zero bearing on worthiness. God intentionally chose her for His unique role. His requirements included an acknowledgment and sorrow for her sins and the need for a Savior. With a humble heart, she pledged obedience in response to His call and plan after she acknowledged her acceptance and need for a Savior to forgive her sins.

Not only the birth of Jesus but also every single detail of his entire life, death, and resurrection fulfilled each Old Testament prophecy in scripture written thousands of years before. This included the miraculous choice of a young virgin as His earthly mother. His life was lived perfectly so we could receive the miraculous gift of merciful salvation.

Have you ever thought about how wonderful it was that Jesus stepped out of eternity into time through a humble virgin's womb in a submissive fetal position? He willingly became utterly dependent upon His earthly parents as a baby to experience everything we have to face. Yet He never sinned.

Questions on The Quest

- Name a time you've been so hungry that you ate anything to quiet the growls and stop the empty sensation? Why were you so hungry?

- Have you ever eaten a food that wasn't the best choice? If so, what was it?

- How long did it take until you felt better?

- Have you ever tried to fill your spiritual hunger with everything but God's life-satisfying Word? If so, how?

PART THREE

MERCY MATERIALIZED

7

MOLDED

About the same time I became a first-time mom, I was invited to attend a weekly women's Bible study through AGLOW Women's Ministries. It was being launched in Kay's neighborhood; she was a dear friend of mine. The gathering included women of all ages from a vast array of faith backgrounds, including a cute little nun. Since Kim was the only child, she was overwhelmingly welcomed and joined me on her little blanket. This group of small beginnings grew exponentially under the committed co-leadership of Kay and Fay, her next-door neighbor.

Hundreds of women and even more children from babies through teens were spiritually fed through relevant topical Bible studies and age-appropriate programs for the children. The group expanded from the home location to a church hall, sanctuary, and cafeteria generously provided by supportive and encouraging pastors in that area over four decades. Many women grew in their faith and relationship with Christ. It became a vital part of my life that God used to gently mold me as His vessel in my home and community. Every week, I looked forward to attending to learn, grow, and appreciate God's relevant *Word* of truth.

It seemed regardless of the subject matter prayerfully chosen by Kay and Fay, God would always provide a personal practical study that mirrored the topic for me to learn firsthand. I vividly recall one particular situation when we were studying the fruits of the Holy Spirit. One Tuesday morning, we had focused on the fruit of peace, and I found myself immediately tested when driving home from the meeting.

That morning before leaving home for the study, I started preparing homemade spaghetti sauce by thawing a pound of ground beef in a double-boiler pan. I turned the dial to the lowest temperature on the front burner of our electric stove. Next, I finished packing a diaper bag and cleaned up breakfast from both of our children. Then, we went out to the car where I buckled them in their car seats and drove to the Bible study. I really enjoyed this teaching on peace and could not wait to test this out when the next opportunity arose.

Ironically, as I drove back home, I noticed in my rear-view mirror that both Kim and Kary had fallen asleep. A sweet expression of peace settled on both of their faces. When I turned onto the entrance of our sub-division, I was quite puzzled why the street was closed off. I drove toward the uniformed captain on guard and let him know I lived down the street, and I asked him if I could pass through to get home to put the children down for their naps. He asked me for my address with proof from my driver's license. After I showed him, he moved the barricade and said he would escort me with his vehicle in the lead.

As I neared our street, I saw our home surrounded by dancing billows of black smoke but still intact. Every door and window were opened. Firefighters in full gear walked in and out of our dwelling and around the yard with calculated precision. At that moment, I was flooded supernaturally with God's peace as many scriptures shared earlier in the day during the Bible study filled my mind. Slowly, I exited the car and followed closely behind the captain through the front door and into our kitchen. Unconsciously, I covered my mouth so I could breathe.

The fireman on site asked if I left something cooking on the stove earlier that morning. I nodded. Then, I further explained it was a double-boiler pan with water in the bottom and frozen ground beef in the top that was covered tightly and set on low heat three hours earlier. I showed him which burner I used. Fine black soot coated every surface in the kitchen. It suddenly struck me that our home could have caught fire and burned instead of this strange scenario. Complete peace enveloped me as I truly understood at that moment it was God's miraculous protection and divine intervention that affected the outcome positively.

Along the subdivision street, neighbors and strangers lined the property edge. Each seemed mesmerized by the eerie smoking sight. The onlookers exchanged occasional chatter as they watched the smoke pour from our home. As I walked out the front door, it seemed that everyone stopped talking and fixed their gaze in my direction. My voice began softly and increased in volume. I was excited to thank God aloud for His protection, peace, and preservation. Many chimed in as well, and they began hugging me and each other. A number of the neighborhood women offered their homes for us to stay in during the future cleanup and restoration. I knew without a doubt God had extended His mercy to me and our family in this very visible way.

A few months later after our kitchen was repainted and restored, our family was able to extend hospitality once again. We volunteered to become personally involved with a displaced Vietnamese refugee family. In the mid-seventies, there was an ongoing sponsorship program nationwide throughout the Catholic Church. Our congregation, St. Gregory the Great, was matched with Chinh, a father, his brother, and three young teenaged sons who all flew to Wisconsin from the refugee camp. The church body provided a furnished apartment with rent paid for one year and employment opportunities for all five.

The goal was for the family to become self-sufficient within one year. Then, the rest of their family who remained in the refugee camp could join them. The rest of their family consisted of Chinh's elderly mother-in-law, his wife, their young son, and two daughters. We were excited to sign up to host the family of men on a Saturday afternoon and evening for a meal and time together.

Mike and I tried to imagine how hard it was for each of them to be separated from their family for an indefinite period of time. On that day, a parishioner drove them to our home around 2:00 p.m. and stated he would return at 8:30 p.m. to bring them back to their apartment.

This was our first experience interacting with an Asian family that had a limited English vocabulary. Almost every night after work was over, this family would be driven to someone's home from the church who volunteered for meal preparation and partake in stiff conversations. After they arrived at our home, only a few minutes of awkward silence passed between us. We felt God wanted us to be ourselves and let them be themselves. Our two little ones broke the ice, bringing their toys and books to interact with the younger two teens. These boys had been missing their younger siblings and immediately got down on the floor for one-on-one playtime despite the slight language barrier.

Mike had the idea to invite our best friend neighbors, Bev and Gary, over for a crazy plan. Gary lent us his small fishing boat strapped on his trailer that Mike hooked up to our riding lawn mower. I'm not exactly sure why, but Mike asked the father if he and his brother and sons would like to go in the boat and be pulled around with the lawn mower throughout the subdivision.

The father was ecstatic and spoke in Vietnamese to tell his family members the bizarre plan. They all got excited and got into the boat with Mike and Gary's assistance. Up and down the streets, this unlikely parade float traveled. Different neighbors came out of their homes and waved warmly. Most everyone knew Mike and Gary's antics were normal in this subdivision.

In the meantime, I finished meal preparations with Bev and had everything ready when the ride was over. As the men came in to wash their hands, they were all so relaxed and genuinely happy. The father and Mike both prayed before the meal in Vietnamese and English, which was another bonding experience for all of us as we held hands together. Dessert was shared later in the family room. We had a small portable organ in that room that one of the sons pointed to, indicating he could play. Beautiful sounds came from his talented fingers as tears began to well in him and many of us. His father shared that he often played a piano in their home for the family now separated but not forgotten. That night, he felt connected to them.

This unique experience for our family laid the foundation to welcome future strangers in our midst to recognize and appreciate the similarities shared rather than fear the differences. Each of us was being molded into a vessel of mercy by the Divine Potter and Creator.

8

MOTIVATED

Three moves later, our family had grown with the blessings of two more biological children, one semi-permanent child, and daily child care for an additional eight children. For the next four years, we decided as a family to remove the TV from our home to create a more nurturing environment for all the children. Instead, creativity, imagination, playing games, cooking/baking, backyard play, reading books, and going to the park many times each week replaced the mundane screen. Involvement at the children's school, scouts, children's Bible study, and in the community rounded out each week. Little by little, all the children, ours and those we cared for, were introduced to regular volunteering. Each became more cognizant of the many opportunities to pray for and extend mercy to relatives, the neighbors, people they knew who suffered physically or mentally, other individuals from churches, or often strangers in the community until it became a natural part of life.

I was introduced to a book titled *The Power of the Praying Parent*, written by Stormie Omartian, which kept me involved prayerfully for all of our children and those who spent extended time with us. Her topics for prayer covered areas I had not ever considered, and I know they were effective in all of the children's early spiritual formation. To this day, I'm truly grateful for her series of books of prayer, which transitioned as our children became older to *Praying For Your Adult Children.*

Our early decision to attend a loving Christian Missionary and Alliance Bible Church in Waukesha gave us the opportunity to also become introduced to a local Bible college called New Tribes. One particular family of four introduced us to their life in and off the mission field of Papua, New Guinea. They invited us to an afternoon dinner at their apartment in the main building. I noticed many makeshift walls in place to separate the bedrooms from the kitchen and eating space. Curiously, there was no running water or bathrooms either. Both were accessible down a long hallway. This was intentional to help students understand future mission placements may not have running water or electricity.

Their adaptability to a simple life, trust in God, and displays of mercy and compassion to a tribal people across the ocean truly impacted all of us. The Wood family explained what a commitment to missions looked like practically, spiritually, emotionally, physically, and relationally too. We had so many questions, and they answered all of them.

Our initial interest grew to a firm decision to attend the training college in Wisconsin for two years, then language school in Missouri for another year. The final goal was to become dorm parents to other missionary parents' children in a foreign country. We were motivated for God to use us as a family. This step of faith became real as we gave some of our possessions away. This was the first step we took to downsize our home for the small apartment living ahead. The requirement to enter debt-free also meant selling our home. We knew God could help us sell our home within a day. The price was right and the housing market stable, so we contracted with a broker and out went the for-sale sign.

Keeping the home orderly for showings was challenging, as I was providing childcare for many children of all ages during this time. Our timeline to sell was three months before the fall term began. We knew no exceptions could be made to the financial requirements of the school and trusted God to bring a buyer.

Three months passed too quickly without any offers at all. Our disappointment arose and so did the questions. Why God didn't want us to serve Him and others at this time? Were our motives wrong? We felt quite unworthy. Yet God, in His mercy and wisdom, had a different plan that would unfold in each of our lives to impact others locally and globally.

About seven months later on one unforgettable day, a Salvation Army staff member called to ask our family to consider taking a Saturday shift at their men's homeless shelter to prepare and serve two meals to the residents. The meals would be preplanned with recipes available and ingredients purchased ahead of time by the regular staff. They wanted to relieve the permanent house parents so they could visit out-of-state family on a well-deserved vacation. All the slots for the week were filled by other volunteers with the exception of the 11:00 a.m. to 7:00 p.m. Saturday shift.

We had visited the shelter briefly a few times in the past year when we dropped off homemade baked treats for the appreciative residents and staff. It was also enjoyable connecting with the captain and his family at various community events. This request was something we could all do as a family and looked forward to fulfilling this one-time commitment.

At the shelter, Saturdays and Sundays were the only day the men didn't have to leave early in the morning to seek employment. If they weren't working on the weekend, they were welcome to stay at the shelter and relax once beds were made and chores completed. We arrived at 10: 45 a.m. to relieve the morning volunteers and familiarize ourselves with the kitchen set-up, recipes, and appliances. Our children were encouraged to be pleasant and kind to the residents, but they always stayed within our view.

One soft-spoken man who said his name was "Peter" offered help if we needed any large pots carried or plates and silverware set up. We appreciated his kindness and let him know we'd call him over. He went to his room and returned with an interesting project he was working on. Peter sat squarely in a wooden chair and meticulously lined up various blue-colored fibers on the top of a small table outside the kitchen. Next, he took two long crochet needles to continue crocheting a rounded vase that surrounded five crocheted lavender flowers attached to dark green crocheted stems. His large fingers incorporated more blue fibers as he crafted the delicate vase effortlessly.

This beautiful creation intrigued all of us but especially Mike. He asked Peter where he learned his craft and was surprised when Peter answered it was when he served a long prison term. I overheard his response and was as curious as Mike was to find out the reason behind his incarceration since this man didn't seem capable of any crime.

Peter shared that eighteen years ago he decided to burglarize a home in a rural Wisconsin area. He entered the place through an unlocked back door and began to strategize what he'd take based on the value of available items. However, he didn't anticipate being interrupted by the homeowners, a humble retired missionary couple in their early sixties. Impulsively, without any regard for the couple, Peter stated he had raped Violet in front of her husband, Leo, and then killed him. Law enforcement from many neighboring communities arrived to find Peter remorseful and the elderly wife extending compassion to him. He said right after he had taken her husband's life, this loving woman, despite her own ache and pain of losing her spouse and being forcibly raped by him, shared with Peter how he could receive God's mercy and forgiveness through the death and resurrection of His son, Jesus Christ.

Peter was so amazed because of her response to him. At the trial, she also asked the judge for leniency instead of a life sentence, which the judge honored. Peter stated that she wrote him in prison bi-weekly, which was the reason he asked Jesus into his life as His Lord and Savior. She sent him Bible studies to challenge him to grow as a new believer. When he was almost done serving his seventeen-year sentence, Violet sent her final letter. She felt that the relationship they had over the many years was to encourage him in his walk with Christ. She extended mercy to him exactly as God did. Peter needed to develop his own support system and find a church family to continue growing. He honored her decision but was visibly grieved by her absence from his life.

He caused death but became alive on this earth and for eternity. His empty life was filled with hope. What could have been the worst day in someone's life God totally transformed. He used a most unlikely frail woman to break through a hardened heart.

It was difficult to hear and comprehend Peter's account, yet Mike and I were changed by God that day through

Peter's redemption story. Peter choked with emotion when he shared about God's forgiveness and mercy. It touched our lives with a desire and the motivation to extend that kind of mercy to those homeless men who were hopeless. We weren't sure how or when but knew God had more on the horizon for all of us beyond serving lunch and dinner on a quiet Saturday afternoon.

At the end of the summer in 1987, our pastor's wife, Wendy, and I decided we would embark on some weight-training exercise. It was offered for three weeks at no cost at the nearby YWCA. Although she was a few years older, Wendy was very energetic and fun and looked stunning in her electric blue stretch pants. This was a new venture for me, so I cautiously examined all the available machines and followed her lead. She sprinted from machine to machine, adding varying weights to increase the resistance without even breaking a sweat. I marveled at her agility and admired her for what she was able to accomplish. We went about forty minutes twice a week.

Early one morning, I had an upsetting dream that woke me up with a racing heart. At least, that was the scenario I thought happened. Mike had already left for work, and I needed to get up so I could feed the four kids and drive them to school. I couldn't, though. I couldn't remember how to get out of bed. My left leg felt heavy, and I had difficulty carrying out our daily routine.

I asked the children to help me get the phone to call Wendy and Pastor Phil to request transportation for school and the doctor. Though I had some difficulty speaking, I dismissed the garbled words, thinking I had tried to speak too quickly. Kim and Kary helped get their younger siblings fed and ready for school. Pastor Phil arrived and kindly drove them in his car. Wendy came a short time later. *Beep*, pause, and *beep beep* again. The walls and carpet swayed in motion. I couldn't put equal weight on my right foot. That shoe felt heavier for some reason. I sat on the top stair of our carpeted stairs trying to figure out how I would walk down them to the front door. Strange feelings and sensations clouded my mind and affected my gait, hand, and arm as Wendy came inside and realized I really wasn't able to walk alone.

A few days later, all the tests were completed, and I was diagnosed with having two separate mini-strokes at age thirty-seven. They were the result of a heart condition and released blood clots while weightlifting. Some residuals remained after the first ten days, including some impaired speech that lasted for a few weeks. My in-home childcare was put on hold for two months.

Many women from the church were so helpful and assisted daily with meals, cleaning, ironing, and transportation for the children. Through their extensive love, mercy, and unselfishness, our situation was resolved in a few weeks. After impacting our lives, this informal group of women became more organized into a vital ministry extension of the church, serving the needs of singles and families experiencing unexpected health crises and other overwhelming situations.

9

MISSIONED

Life returned to our normal pace after only a few months. The following summer, I noticed a small ad in the local newspaper for a part-time social worker position at the Salvation Army that would begin in the fall. We had previously volunteered there, so I felt like this would be a great new direction to take. The hours seemed as though they would work since all four of our children would begin full-time school for the first time.

Only weeks before this ad was placed, we said our sad goodbyes to Richard and Mary. Her father was experiencing poor health, and Mary knew it was time to return to her family home to assist her mom in providing care for him. She also knew Richard would enjoy his special grandpa time. The other children we cared for in the home had also moved away or grew up and no longer needed after school or summer care.

I applied for the position, even though I felt so inadequate to fulfill the role of a case manager social worker. After retrieving and reviewing some outdated sociology textbooks and materials, I realized preparation for this specific position was pointless. Instead, comforting thoughts reminded me regarding each past experience in life's journey, God always equipped me with whatever I needed at the time. That's how my faith in Him grew.

Why couldn't I trust Him in working with homeless men? Soon, I would learn that most clients came to the shelter with drug and alcohol addictions, criminal records, and dual diagnoses of combined mental health issues. I'd also realize that my past experience of nurturing dozens and dozens of children through the years was the right practical knowledge I could implement daily with the varying personalities of men of all ages and education.

Initially, I was deeply troubled by the cursing, rough, and vulgar language that was shared quite commonly at the intake by prospective residents. At first, it was a huge challenge. I hadn't been in the workforce for over fourteen years. In our home, the words *dumb* or *stupid* were intolerable *bad* words for our children or those we watched. Those were words not to be used in our home or outside playing, and they thoroughly respected these rules.

At the shelter and in the office, those taking God's name so callously in vain hurt my heart and ears. Could I continue? I prayed, "Holy Spirit, confirm to me that you want me to stay in this position. Help me to extend mercy to each man, especially when it is so difficult." One by one, each of my male clients began to apologize if they used God's name in vain, swore, or began to use a vulgar word around me. Many would begin attending the Sunday and weekday services offered to the residents, though not required by the Salvation Army Corps.

So many of my clients had visible and spiritual trans-formations during the twelve weeks they were allowed to stay in the shelter. Some continued attending the Salvation Army Church long after they were discharged and back on their feet. It was because of an eternal and internal difference that happened, resulting in a new direction for their lives.

Six months after they hired me, Captain Braddock, the officer in charge of the Corps, and also my boss, asked me if Mike enjoyed his position as a sheet metal journeyman. I knew Mike worked at the factory to support all of us but wasn't planning on staying with the company forever. My frequent response to Captain was that Mike is always open to God's will. Captain only smiled and went on with his work. Little did Mike or I know, God was always working behind the scenes so we would be able to experience full-time vocational ministry as a family.

During this time, I learned so many things about being a social worker at the Salvation Army I couldn't find in any textbook. This was on-the-job training at its best under the able tutelage of the Holy Spirit and a gifted supervisor named Julie Cervantes. My contacts and connections in the community grew and included law enforcement, the correctional system, and local medical entities. I loved this position and realized being a

- cheerleader AKA encourager
- mom AKA compassionate
- older sister AKA listener
- and social worker AKA resource and referral specialist

were roles of support lacking in many of the men's lives. I had first-hand experience in all of those areas and enjoyed networking on behalf of my clients.

Early on, I learned two major lessons that impacted me. The first was after reading an article with this poignant poem that follows:

I can't hear your words, man
about some God hanging on a tree.
My belly's making fearful sounds that
drown out what you say.

And I can't understand your story,
'cause I'm so cold and scared,
too busy chasing shadows in my head
to listen to what you say.

Seems I heard that song before
about how much God loves me.
But till you show me that you care
I can't hear a word you say.

—© 1988, Sandra Higgs[1]

The second was discovering that the greatest need from many of the homeless men I interviewed was socks. It was true! A pair of socks could satisfy their greatest need in that moment of time. I often stopped an intake interview and took out two pair of new tube socks from my bottom desk drawer, offering them a new pair whether the man was going to stay as a resident and follow all the rules or not. An ongoing stock was maintained in all sizes that I purchased on sale with our family's budgeted grocery money. Time and time again, God always seemed to replenish our funds after we purchased more men's socks.

I loved hearing new residents personal accounts of generous acts of kindness they received from other residents.

---

[1] Reprinted with permission from *Alliance Life Magazine*, January 18, 1989.

Tears often welled in my eyes as a new resident shared how another resident made them feel welcome to the shelter home and family by kindly sharing a laundered pair of socks from their own locked cupboard. A continuous cycle of mercy was repeated among the men throughout my days there. Pairs of socks received and then given to another were often the first steps that began the internal changes in hearts and souls too.

Within eight months of being hired, our staff welcomed Mike, my favorite co-worker! Captain Braddock worked out the perfect position for him as Director of Outreach Programs. However, this role required us to become members (Soldiers) of the Salvation Army Church and leave our loving, nurturing Christian and Missionary Alliance Church we treasured dearly.

Pastor Phil and Mike had become very close. Phil was like a third father to him after his own and my dad.

He gave him wise counsel and also his full blessing if Mike decided to accept the position. It meant taking a significant pay cut in salary. This decision involving our whole family needed prayerful consideration, discernment, and faith. We knew God would show us, and we were all willing to follow His lead.

We decided to sell one car, which in turn, meant a lower insurance rate. The private Christian school our children all attended had a policy that if both parents were involved in ministry, then the tuition would be half the regular cost. Although we were unaware of this benefit, God was fully cognizant. These two changes resulted in significant monthly savings.

We were ready to commit 100%. Suddenly, we understood why our home hadn't sold to begin training at New Tribes for global mission work. Our mission field was in sight within our own community, and God had been training us all along. Pastor Phil and Wendy coordinated a beautiful church service of farewell and encouragement. He recognized we were called by God, and they affirmed their love and prayer support of our family as local missionaries in our community.

In the summer one year later, our fifteen-year-old daughter, Kim, attended a teen conference in Colorado with the former church youth group. The conference held every third year was called LIFE. At that time, God revealed Himself to her in a deeper way, and she responded wholly. She signed and dated a small card she still carries that is pictured on the next page.

THE CHRISTIAN AND
MISSIONARY ALLIANCE

I commit myself to serve the Lord in a
full-time Christian vocation. Unless He
should clearly lead otherwise, I will
keep my commitment by His grace.

Date   Signature

The stirring in her heart that began that day continues decades later. She began attending New Tribes (now called Ethnos 360 Bible Institute) in 1992 and, in the years that followed, prepared for cross-cultural service in a number of ways. She attended Grace College in Indiana to earn her teaching degree.

Her personal journey of dedication and surrender has allowed her to extend mercy and influence the lives of people of all ages and backgrounds, both domestically and internationally.

MERCY MOMENT OF TRUTH

My Life Verse

… Lo, I am with you always, even unto the end of the age.

—Matthew 28:20 (NKJV)

This portion of the final scripture verse located at the end of the book of Matthew is a core life truth for me. These thirteen words have been a lifeline to me in dark hours, joy moments, thousands of feet in the air above oceans and mountains, in a prison cell ministering, at the delivery of a baby, behind a waterfall, next to a casket, during courtroom interrogation, and when receiving anesthesia before surgery. In each instance, the power, hope, and comfort of those thirteen words becomes almost unexplainable.

I'm not certain of the first time I embraced this scripture, but it had to be at least three decades before. In some versions of the Bible, this portion begins with the words surely or behold. But when I came upon "Lo, I am with you always …" something powerful stirred in my soul. I felt as though God addressed me personally with my initials, L and O, or Lo. Initially, I pondered each individual word. Then, I followed with reflection in awe and awareness of the full magnitude of the verbiage. The truth, depth, and promise of this verse had me soaring.

It was and is overwhelming to think that God, who created the universe with His Word, would have the time or desire to be ever present in my life, always extending His undeserved mercy. Contrarily, at times, I choose to allow distractions, substitutes, and meaningless diversions occupy my time and mind.

God's Word is alive and active, similar to a firmly held sharp two-edged sword. His Word discerns the thoughts and intentions of each heart, meaning we won't be able to make excuses for our behaviors and choices. Instead, we become exposed as intended, and the result is a purposeful life lived without guilt, shame, or regret.

Reflections on The Quest

- Reflect upon a time when you felt completely out of God's reach. What were the circumstances?

- Have you ever felt beyond God's forgiveness? Was this feeling true or false? How do you know?

- Has a Bible verse ever spoke to your personal situation in a unique way? If so, what were the circumstances?

PART FOUR

MERCY MOBILIZED

10

MINISTERED

"Frontline Battle or Ministry" was an accurate phrase our family quickly acquainted ourselves with after I committed to work full-time. We experienced it previously to a lesser degree when we operated *The Apple of His Eye* Christian Book and Gift Store.

In this setting at the homeless shelter plus the additional Army Corps activities of daycare, seniors, meal program, Bible studies, food pantry, the annual Christmas toy distribution, kettle and bell-ringing campaign, and more, there was a direct correlation between major breakthroughs in clients' lives and the amount of persecution and strife to the staff, organization, and leadership families. This spiritual warfare took place in many ways with attacks on relationships, health, and finances. This often manifested in violence, slander, vandalism, deceit, rebellion, theft, and verbal and physical assaults.

The first line of defense was to always trust God in combination with prayer. It was also important to respond with mercy, forgiveness, and grace at all times. Standing firm and deciding not to personally compromise unwavering faith in Jesus Christ was a challenge through many horrendous circumstances and evil situations that occurred.

Without a doubt, we knew each person, food pantry client, homeless man, or family who walked through the doors was sent by God for His purpose that He would often reveal. One young Caucasian man with a crisply ironed shirt sat in the waiting room. He bent his neck forward and cradled his head in his hands.

So many of the homeless clients came in with an unkempt appearance and distinguishable odor indicating they had not been able to shower for a while. Each person mattered and was valued at the Salvation Army. To me, listening to every story was a privilege.

One day, our volunteer receptionist had a medical appointment, so my co-worker, Peggy, and I came from the back offices to the front to meet our next client. Usually, everyone who came in for any services would place their first name, or whatever name they used that day, on a waiting list.

I grabbed the clipboard and noticed all the names were already crossed off since they had been served. This young man was next and the only remaining person in the quiet room. But no name was written down. My heart was already feeling his pain. I walked over, squatted down a little, and introduced myself. He slowly dropped his arms and hands. With tear stains on his cheeks and reddened eyes, he avoided direct eye contact with me. I grabbed some tissues from the desk and handed them to him, and he used them immediately.

After getting him a glass of water and inviting him to sit down in my office, he said he had been permanently kicked out of his girlfriend's home, was not in communication any longer with his family, and never thought he would find himself in need of a homeless shelter.

After he composed himself and said he felt better, the intake began. However, after giving his name and age, I was in tears as I hugged this young man. Then, I called Mike on the intercom to also come to our building for a hug. Unknowingly, he was a child I babysat for during a three-year period at our home along with his brother and sister many years before. One of his parents had died unexpectedly at an early age four years before, and that had devastated him. Since the death, he made many bad decisions trying to numb his pain of grief and loss.

During Jason's eight-week stay at the shelter over the glorious Easter season, he found a new beginning in Christ as his Savior, changed the direction of his life for eternity, stopped drinking, and initiated a plan to receive grief counseling from a licensed therapist. He began to personally understand the meaning behind mercy and reconciliation. This revelation was necessary for him to reconnect with close family members that were estranged.

After apologizing to his former boss, Jason was rehired in the well-paying position he loved. His abilities to save money and implement life skills were already in place. When Jason was ready to leave the shelter, it was difficult for Mike and me to say goodbye but knew he was well-equipped for all his next chapters in life.

So many of the clients impacted us as a family both positively and some negatively with lessons learned for future ministry. Some relationships of deep and valued friendship continue throughout our lives.

One remarkable client who impacted our entire family forever was Johnny Orosco. He initially called from a hospital-based drug and alcohol rehab program he had successfully completed that morning. He inquired if a bed was available for him at the shelter. One was and would be held for him for four hours until the rehab program driver could drop him off for his intake. He was so excited a bed was available. His joy was a bit contagious as he said in a heavy Puerto Rican accent, "I am starting my life again at the Salbation Army." He pronounced the "v" as a "b," which made me smile.

A short time later, a man in his forties walked in the main door. He was sweating and clutched his chest falling into a chair and dropping his bag of belongings next to him. I ran to his side to help this distressed stranger. I got a glass of water and a cold washcloth and watched him gasp for breath. He gave all the seated clients in the reception area quite a scare. Slowly, he sipped the water as I placed the cloth on his head. I waited to see if an ambulance was needed. Then, the sweating man said, "I'm Johnny, and the hill I just walked up to get here was very steep. I'm not going to do that again." Then, he let out a belly laugh that put everyone at ease. He said he needed his heart medication from his bag that he brought with him. Unfortunately, he noticed it wasn't in there as he sifted through the contents. He took some deep breaths and asked if I could drive him back to the rehab center to retrieve all his medications he left behind.

As I drove to the rehab center with Johnny in the agency van, I felt this nudge and whisper from God to take extra care of this guy during his time at the shelter. As I listened to Johnny's story of his past forty days, I realized how God had miraculously spared his life. What I didn't know was how God in His unlimited mercy would restore this man and use him to touch hearts and souls in Wisconsin, New York, Texas, Florida, and Puerto Rico.

Johnny was weak because one of his main heart valves was replaced with a pig's valve a few years before. He had been heavily involved with drugs, particularly cocaine. Johnny used, bought, and sold for years. Previously,

Johnny had served hard time for quite a few years in Ryker's Prison in New York. Among many drug charges, he had also taken another man's life. He was on probation in Waukesha; however, he continued to sell cocaine in the downtown area to support his own habit.

He acknowledged that his probation officer tried to work with him and always gave him another chance. After one weekend of continual drug use and no sleep for over thirty hours, Johnny said he felt very sick and walked down the dark hall to the rooming house shower where he lived. It was shared by all the boarders living above the popular bar. He isn't sure what happened but knew he lost consciousness. When he opened his eyes briefly while sprawled on the floor, he decided he no longer wanted to live anymore and closed them for one last time.

"Plink, plink, plink," he demonstrated on his face adding, "many more plinking cool, wet, liquid drops followed." He continued his story. "I knew someone turned water on me that felt like raindrops hitting my face and body. I tried to get up slowly, not knowing who turned on the shower. I realized at that moment I wanted to live, really live, but no longer on drugs."

He was hospitalized for his heart condition, dehydration, and poor nutrition and called his probation officer from his hospital room. His mind was clear. He had hope and the will to live again. Johnny asked him for one more chance and the opportunity to enter the twenty-one-day hospital rehab program that was now possible because he was already an inpatient.

The day we met him was the day he graduated ready to begin his next chapter at the "Salbation Army." The first Sunday after his arrival, he came early to attend the church service with our family. In the front of the church, a long rail extended across the altar with an area in front to kneel. It's actually called the *Mercy Seat* and available for the purpose of personal repentance, forgiveness, mercy, and restoration. Johnny, without prompting from anyone, went forward and knelt down midway through the service. He poured out his heart to God in repentance and gratefulness even crying aloud. Johnny shared it was that day when he first experienced God's mercy and newfound joy. Over the next few months, I witnessed a profound transformation in his life.

He met often in Mike's office because he wanted to learn from him about God's Word. Johnny always helped out and volunteered in any way he physically could, ministering to many clients of all ages. Although we were all the same age, Johnny always referred to Mike and me as his spiritual momma and papa, which felt truly humbling.

The fruit of God living and dwelling in Johnny was manifested as he sought forgiveness from people he had hurt or caused pain to in his past. Many years before, he left New York after abandoning his girlfriend and the son he had fathered. On Mother's Day after an impacting sermon, Johnny asked to use my office phone for a long-distance call he needed to make to New York. I agreed, knowing he intended to reconcile with someone. He contacted Noemi, his son's mother, apologizing she had to raise their son as a single mother for so many years. She forgave him and let him know she had been praying for him for a number of years after becoming a Christian and growing in her faith.

That phone call began a restored relationship. Numerous calls between them continued for many months. In response, Noemi left the streets of Brooklyn, New York, with her son and a younger daughter to resettle in the sleepy city of Waukesha. She and Johnny dated, prayed together, and became involved at a Hispanic church. They counseled with their Pastor and then knew it was the right time to get married. Mike, me, and our daughter, Sarah, were asked to stand up in their wedding. We felt honored to be part of such a glorious day of union and testimony to their families and the community.

Their love was beautiful as God used them in Wisconsin for prison ministry a few years until both Noemi and Johnny's health conditions grew worse in the cold Wisconsin winters. They moved to Florida where some of Noemi's relatives lived about an hour south of Orlando. Johnny and Noemi became involved in their church as Johnny discipled men in the group he led, visited the imprisoned, and gave his testimony to whomever would listen. Together, they visited the sick, were part of the worship ministry, and befriended the unlovable. Whenever they visited Wisconsin, we got together for some quality time.

Johnny's last twenty-three years of his life were lived with godly intent and eternal purpose, never saying no to any request for his time or prayer. He lived life as a grandfather of six and spiritual papa to hundreds. On April 9, 2014, Noemi called in tears to share that Johnny's heart suddenly stopped beating that day. She said he didn't suffer but had been in his recliner reading his Bible. Ever so gently, his open Bible rested on his chest as he closed his eyes for the last time. Noemi was heartbroken but knew Johnny would want her to minister for both of them. She continues to devote her time to minister God's love and mercy to many people in Florida, on annual mission trips to Mexico and Honduras, Wisconsin when she is able to visit, and wherever else God leads.

After doing Johnny's intake years before, I always appreciated each unique client and their story. Tears, struggles, joy, frustration, laughter, disappointment, sweat, death, pain, birth, miracles, and defeat all became the essence of my days. Each interaction fueled my passion to extend mercy. I began to recognize only God could use what little I offered to the clients for His eternal purposes.

Celebrating the victories, witnessing life transformations, and hearing numerous testimonies of boys, girls, teens, adults, and seniors made this season well worth the family investment of seven plus years of our lives until Mike had an unexpected heart attack at age forty-one. That was an obvious cue it was time for us to leave that ministry and make sure Mike got the healing and rest he needed.

At the time of our departure from the Salvation Army, I was simultaneously employed elsewhere in two part-time positions. I thoroughly enjoyed both because I could exercise my compassion and also passion to extend mercy. One position was at the Waukesha County Jail and Federal Prison as a contracted psychiatric social worker.

* * *

100

My role there was to meet with every incarcerated inmate, both male and female, to determine their mental health status for a national certification process. A signature was required from each inmate indicating they were offered mental health counseling and an assessment within the first five days of their admission. If there were indications an individual should see the staff psychiatrist, a referral was made. Secondly, if any inmate was thought to be suicidal, I needed to meet with them immediately. Although I was hired in this secular position to meet the certification requirements, God allowed me to obtain permission and favor to share spiritual encouragement and materials with the inmates unless they were hostile or refused. Refusals were minimal, which I fully respected.

Truthfully, I did not feel qualified for the position. It allowed me a whole new level to trust God since I often had to meet with some intimidating individuals in a holding cell or bullpen immediately after they were booked. I had to assess and approve each of them for safety and admission to the general population or another more appropriate cell or pod. Each secured cell was opened for me from a central control room. Then, I was locked in and took a seat either next to the individual or directly across from the inmate on the cold, bare, metal ledge. I always brought my yellow pad of paper, a Chick bible cartoon tract minus the staples (see definition of Chick tract in "Notes" at the end of this book), two business cards of mine, a few tissues, and a pen. Suspected murderers, rapists, armed robbers, and other perpetrators were inmates brought in for this initial assessment. Never once did I carry pepper spray or a staff radio that the correctional officers all carried.

Instead, God fully equipped me with His mercy to see the lostness of each soul before me. He gave me discernment to determine the appropriate placement and favor to connect with that person to understand how I could pray for them. Before concluding most of the interviews, tissues were offered and accepted. Almost every person wanted to keep the Chick tract that I was delighted to share. Some asked for additional counseling sessions and wrote my name and reason on a request form. I provided

Biblical counseling for two sessions, then suggested an outside referral to one of the jail-approved pastors whom I knew would be a good fit.

* * *

The other part-time position was as an adoption home study social worker contracted with the Evangelical Child and Family Agency (ECFA). The ECFA prospective adoptive couples and families I met with to interview for home studies were stable and such a delight to know. Their life stories and biographies balanced out the dysfunctional stories of other clients I heard daily. In addition, the narratives shared by some of the couples educated me on the difficulty, heartache, and sadness when they experienced infertility and miscarriages.

In my early days at ECFA, all home studies and reports were generated from one massive agency electric typewriter. The staff secretary produced most of the final drafts. She was proficient at grammar, use of tense, court terminology, and typing with lightning speed. She was wise, kind, quite a character, and maternally hearted. Her name was Kit, and no one was ever allowed to know her age. She loved Jesus first in her life and then her family yet somehow made immediate room in her heart for everyone else she met.

On October 18, 1994, my dad died suddenly at the age of sixty-eight. Only ten weeks before, he casually mentioned a small lump in his jawline to the doctor treating my mom for cancer. Her doctor biopsied my dad's lump during her appointment since he was immediately concerned it was cancerous. It was. A few days later, the physician removed some surrounding suspicious tissue. It was unclear if there were additional tumors growing elsewhere.

Two days before he died, he was very weak. He went to his church for the Sunday service and afterward couldn't walk to his car in the parking lot let alone drive home the eight blocks. My brother brought him home and became even more concerned after he put on pajamas with his assistance and crawled in his bed to rest. This was abnormal for an otherwise energetic man. My dad and mom lived in the side-by-side with my brother, John, and wife, Nancy, and family where we used to live with our four children. My brother was troubled by the rapid decline in his health in only a few hours. He called me to spend the remainder of the afternoon with him. Mike realized I should be with him for quality father-daughter time and drove me over right away. I found it hard to believe my dad was so weak and back in his pajamas. My mom was not aware he had cancer. She thought he had a cold since his throat and voice had become raspy. Her physical and cognitive limitations often prevented her from fully grasping the severity of a situation. She peacefully napped in her bedroom on her hospital bed equipped with air and sand to prevent bed sores.

This was difficult for me to see him so frail in such a short period of time. We literally talked for hours that sweet Sunday afternoon. Although he would often take five-minute dozes, they seemed to help him rally and regain some momentum. He continued speaking or asking a question right where he left off.

In those beautiful hours, he often referred to his relationship with Jesus confidently. He wanted me to read him some scripture verses and favorite passages he enjoyed, in particular Psalm 23. Smiling serenely, he acknowledged sensing an overwhelming peace and joy in anticipation for the coming days. His thoughts would then center on others he was in the process of helping or visiting regularly that he wanted to make sure were cared for in the coming weeks in case he became too weak. None of us had any idea how close he was to death. To me, this precious heart-to-heart time with my earthly father was a merciful gift from my heavenly Father to both of us.

That night after I left, my brother took him to the hospital. The next night, I tucked him in bed after a short visit in his hospital room. The medical staff expressed hope that he'd be discharged within a few days and planned to place a gavage feeding tube on his abdomen. They estimated his remaining life to be six months to a year for quality time with the family. He died unexpectedly the following day.

After I left his hospital room seeing his lifeless body, I robotically walked to my car and drove to the ECFA office, only a few blocks away. Kit heard the front office door open and came out to the reception area where I stood trying to stifle my shallow moans in disbelieving sorrow. As soon as she saw my face, she knew what had happened without me saying a word. She encircled her arms around me and held me as I sobbed so hard. She patted my back and repeated, "I'm so sorry. I'm so sorry."

She extended healing mercy to me without limit in that moment of time, even though she didn't know me very well. God truly put her in my life that day as His representative. Through two decades, she became a close confidant and second mother to me until her death in June 2016.

* * *

My full-time employment with ECFA began in July 1995 when an opening for a social worker in the pregnancy support services program coincided with me getting ready for my next challenge in life. My only concern to work full-time in this ministry was that I would be b-o-r-e-d. My experiences with the Salvation Army clients and jail and prison inmates had kept my adrenaline levels quite elevated, which I hoped could continue. God reminded me of His sovereignty in past experiences. He wanted me to trust Him daily.

The treasured journey began in an unexpected way on my first day when my knowledgeable co-worker, Tanya, was taken to the hospital and placed on three months of bedrest that began immediately. She was going to train me before her maternity leave, and I was ready to learn. Evidently, this was no surprise to God. Thankfully, He had been preparing me for years. Once again, it was time for mercy to be mobilized in and through me.

11

MENTORED

After realizing my orientation and training plan to become a pregnancy support services social worker was taking a different trajectory, I recognized this role may not be as boring as I feared. Ron, the director of social services in Wisconsin at ECFA, had already been familiar with my home studies that he signed off on. He initially interviewed me and recommended me for hire in the adoption program a few years before. Immediately, Ron stepped up to mentor me and altered his schedule to provide some of the training I'd need to serve my own caseload of birthparents experiencing an unplanned pregnancy.

I appreciated Ron's direct style and vast experience in the social services field. Discovering he would need to provide some training for me to work with birthparents may not have been plan A. However, Ron graciously took me under his wing to share what he knew. I marveled how well he had organized his office and bookshelves. When he showed me examples of documents I needed to familiarize myself with, I couldn't help noticing how each page was carefully shrouded in its own protective plastic covering. Every individual plastic page was three-hole punched on the side for return and preservation in one of his huge binders.

This man's knowledge was something I admired and wanted to attain so I could effectively help every client in need of services. Ron saw potential in me and patiently imparted many snippets of his wisdom as my first mentor. I also learned it was ok to have personal emotions surface and express them with clients during their times of struggle and also joy. He often pulled out a cloth handkerchief when needed, and I always made sure I carried tissues with me or had a box available for clients I met with in my office.

At ECFA, every person on staff in Wisconsin and at the corporate office in Illinois wanted co-workers to succeed in their positions. Affirmations and encouragement were given freely as well as helpful critique so that staff could improve and implement Christ-honoring services to clients both professionally and personally.

One particular staff member in the Illinois office always had an unmistakable optimistic demeanor and contagious smile. His name was Ken Withrow, and he had been hired years before me at ECFA as a social worker initially serving birthparents.

When I began full time in 1995, Ken was the executive director. He said I had been his first hire in 1991 when he was promoted. Despite the miles between the offices, Ken was my top boss, mentor, and friend the next twenty-two years. I learned verbally and also through observation innumerable things from this man of high character and integrity. He always fulfilled his word because he was (and still is) a man continually invested and immersed in God's Word. His entire adult life has been dedicated to extending mercy and caring for others in his family, the ministry of ECFA, his church, and also the community in his humble way.

Ken also gave me freedom to be who God created me to be, which was often unconventional in the field of social work. He also taught me why paperwork and statistics were a necessary component to effective caseload management. Ken understood when my emotions for clients became out of balance. And he deeply empathized with me when my client's nine-week-old baby suddenly died while in ECFA foster care.

The baby's mother, Claudia, had originally been my client through the Salvation Army position I had in Waukesha. She had a mental health diagnosis, and I had always looked forward to when she would come for a food pantry visit so we could catch up on her life struggles and dreams for her future. On one occasion she commented that she knew she could ask me to be her mentor but wasn't ready for that type of accountability relationship. I chuckled, appreciating her honesty.

Claudia called ECFA one day asking to speak to me. I had been working in the pregnancy support services program for almost three years and truly loved every one of my clients. Each phone call was another opportunity for me to listen to the spoken and unspoken needs of every caller. I also knew God could provide me with enough mercy for each person and situation. As I answered the transferred call, I wasn't certain if anyone was on the other end. Silence continued, then I heard soft sobs on the line.

"Hi, this is Linda. How can I help you?" The quivering voice formed sighing sounds. Then, I strained to hear her hesitant words. "This is Claudia. You already know me. You know, from Salvation Army." Memories of Claudia flooded back immediately. She had been involved with social services and terminated parental rights to her son a few years before through a Voluntary Termination of Parental Rights Hearing. She said, "Can you tell me what you do for your job cause I'm pregnant, and I don't want any county caseworkers in my life?"

Her blatant words confirmed to me it was truly Claudia on the other end. Simultaneously, as she spoke, I felt overwhelming mercy welling up that I wanted to share. I carefully explained my role and the many options available to her for the baby's future. She decided to meet with me as soon as I could. An option shared that appealed to Claudia was the agency's private short-term foster care in the home of one of our licensed Christian families. She needed to have DNA confirmation after the baby was born so that child support could be requested from the birthfather. Her adult rooming house didn't allow children to reside, so alternative placement was necessary, and Claudia preferred knowing where her baby would live instead of having the county make that decision.

It was so good to reconnect with Claudia again. She became accountable to implement goals from a service plan we created together. In one goal, Claudia succeeded to curtail her smoking during the remaining three months of her pregnancy. Fresh fruits and vegetables replaced some processed and junk foods that were previously the mainstay of her diet.

We developed a plan to have the newborn baby placed in an ECFA baby foster home at hospital discharge while they performed DNA testing to determine paternity. The county where Claudia resided also approved this plan since our agency was licensed with the State of Wisconsin for temporary foster placements.

Baby Isabella was born after a very short labor for Claudia on January 21, 1998. In the hospital, Claudia was so joyful interacting with her beautiful baby. I had never seen her this maternal in the past, and I took a few photos of this mother-daughter pair with the agency camera. Our ECFA foster mother would also take photos of Isabella's first weeks for Claudia to cherish.

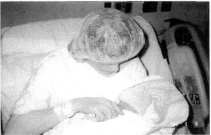

All six of the ECFA licensed Foster Parents were absolute treasures who patiently cared for the babies primarily for the first weeks and months of life. Their purpose was to provide loving, quality, and consistent care before the termination of parental rights hearings, for respite, or other unique case-by-case situations such as Claudia's. These sacrificial families placed their lives on hold. The foster moms and dads cared for the infant during the period when a baby was up at night crying, fussing, and adjusting to formula and days and nights outside the womb. Sometimes a baby would go through withdrawal from cocaine, other drugs, or alcohol, presenting with shrill screams that couldn't be soothed. These families also opened their homes to visits from the placing birthparents to help with their grieving. In addition, they served as mentors to the prospective adoptive couples to teach bathing, feeding, and soothing techniques that would help them connect to that child if and when placement occurred.

On March 12, 1998, I received a call I will never forget. Our deeply saddened foster mother explained she found Baby Isabella dead in her crib when she went to check why she was still sleeping. She had fed her a bottle only a few hours earlier and laid her back to sleep since she was still tired. Now, the medical coroner was at her home. His team took the baby's crib and other items used by Baby Isabella for investigation, which was the protocol in any child's death. They asked me to notify Claudia and ask her permission for an autopsy within the hour. How could I?

Earlier that morning, I had driven down to ECFA's Illinois office with Ron for a meeting. Now, I was hours away from Claudia's rooming house where she rented her one-room efficiency apartment. Ken, my boss and executive director, hugged me, expressing his sorrow and immediately went back to the conference room to lead the other staff in prayer for all those involved.

Thinking about everyone involved caused my whole body to ache. The foster mother sounded devastated. I couldn't imagine what she, her husband, and children would be undergoing in the next few days. Then, I couldn't imagine telling Claudia and prayed for God's mercy for this whole situation. The sixty-minute timeframe was ticking down fast.

My next thought was to call Dave Cruz who was on staff at the police department in that county. He and his wife, Patti, had become dear friends too. His position as the warrant officer combined with his amiable personality allowed him favor and respect in the community from many of the rougher characters and criminals of the city.

People trusted him because he was fair and honest. I asked if he could do the difficult death notification and autopsy request to Claudia within the hour and gave him the info he needed. He was really the only one I trusted to be both compassionate and merciful to Claudia whom he knew well. Without any hesitation, Dave agreed and added, "If there's anything else I can do, let me know anytime of the day or night. And of course, Patti and I will be praying for everyone involved." Dave was a dependable Christian brother I could lean on no matter how bleak a situation seemed.

Baby Isabella's death was a first. There were no manuals or plastic sheets of directions to follow. Instead, I needed to trust God for every detail, and He amply provided. Even though Claudia was deeply saddened, she didn't display any anger or bitterness toward anyone. Instead, she asked how the foster mother was doing with the loss to her and her family. Claudia's response was definitely unexplainable. It was a sign and a true comfort of God's mercy the foster mother received.

Strangely, the same day the baby died was also the day we received the DNA results. It confirmed with 98.9999% probability that Renaldo, an older Hispanic acquaintance of Claudia's, was Baby Isabella's father. He was notified by the county's child support department. Hours later, Claudia sent word to Renaldo through a mutual friend that his baby died, and a funeral was pending after conclusive autopsy results.

Claudia and I had to take care of so many details together that are foreign to most people. We went to the Hartson Funeral Home, which was owned by faithful longtime ECFA donors, Gary and Missy. This husband and wife team graciously treated Claudia with Christ's love, respect, and compassion for her sudden loss. They mercifully said there would be no cost for any of their services and advised us of the next steps for the funeral process. The first item was to locate a church that could host the wake and service followed by confirming a final place for her burial. Together, we picked out a tiny light blue casket that a single pallbearer would carry out after the service concluded. Claudia wanted an open casket to see her baby since she had not visited Isabella in the foster home. Her only memory was in the hospital after she was born when she held her close, fed, and changed her tiny diapers. She also asked if I could take pictures at the funeral to capture and preserve those memories for her.

That afternoon, Claudia and I picked out a beautiful white lacy dress from Wal-Mart. They had their Easter display rack well-stocked with attire for a baby to wear on Easter or for a christening or dedication. We also purchased a baby bonnet with two satiny ribbons that matched perfectly.

Claudia said she had attended First Assembly of God Church in Waukesha on and off for a couple years. She felt comfortable with the pastor and care by some of the women who befriended her in the past and hoped the service could be held there. I called Pastor Verne Hagenbach from First Assembly of God to tell him about Claudia, Baby Isabella, and Renaldo. Pastor Verne genuinely cared about people's souls in the community whether they were members of his church or not. He knew Claudia and immediately agreed to extend mercy and compassion without limit to her, Renaldo, or any family and friends who wanted to attend the service. Sensitively, he also offered to provide a little lunch afterward to the mourners, recognizing most of them rarely sat down to eat a decent meal.

I also contacted Johnny Orosco to see if he could preach a gospel message in Spanish for those who couldn't understand the English service delivered by Pastor Verne. Johnny cried at first and said he'd definitely extend mercy in his message to those of Hispanic background. He acknowledged that he knew Renaldo and his family and welcomed the opportunity.

On the day of the funeral, the pews began to fill up. There were

- Claudia's family
- Renaldo and his family
- Street people
- ECFA staff from Illinois and Wisconsin
- Agency donors and volunteers
- Foster Parents
- County caseworkers
- First Assembly members

and of course, the caring and professional staff from Hartson's Funeral Home.

Claudia was sad and somber and sat in the front row to the right of the open casket that revealed the tiny precious life she bore. It was amazing to look around at the diverse group of people gathered together in one location. Pastor Verne's message combined mercy and truth with an emphasis on comforting Claudia yet clearly sharing only those in a saving relationship would see Baby Isabella again.

When Johnny shared his God-inspired message in his first language, the Hispanic attenders affirmed his words aloud and nodded with *amens*. Many tears flowed from all throughout the service. Johnny asked if anyone wanted that personal relationship with Jesus. Many raised their hands, including Renaldo. After the service, he stepped aside to an adjacent room with a number of the Hispanic people whom he prayed for and followed up with his engaging warmth.

Claudia grew very sorrowful as the casket lid was closed, grabbing my hand in a firm clutch. She said she, too, wanted to see her baby again and knew she wanted to recommit her life to Jesus at that moment. Pastor Verne hadn't heard the conversation but saw the unsettledness in Claudia and asked her if she was ok. At that time, the casket needed to be carried out to the waiting hearse. Everything seemed to be frozen in time. Greg Marris, an ECFA Council Member who arrived late because he was working, walked up to the front pew where we were seated and extended his hand to Claudia. He was an on-duty firefighter and dressed in full uniform, sensitive to the sadness at this moment when time stood still. The navy-blue figure leaned down and respectfully offered to carry the closed casket to the hearse. Claudia slowly looked up at him and nodded affirmatively because she didn't want me to leave her side. Greg's compassion and demeanor were heaven-sent at that moment. The keyboard player began to play a hymn as Greg carried the casket out with noticeable tears upon his face. Pastor Verne knelt next to Claudia and asked what was wrong. She said she knew she wanted her life to be different and wanted to recommit her life to Jesus. Pastor Verne prayed with her. Moments later, another young woman who was Claudia's friend and involved for a few years in prostitution asked for Jesus' forgiveness and began her new life, born again, with Jesus as Pastor Verne prayed.

Years later, I ran into Claudia and didn't actually recognize her at first. She was part of a group of engaging people who were distributing Bible tracts and ministry brochures at an outdoor festival. My curiosity drew me to a large booth that had some uplifting energetic music playing. When I stopped to reach for the brochure she held out, I noticed this church and ministry focus was to those broken by alcohol and drugs. She recognized me first and leaned forward to give me a huge hug. Her face beamed with joy. She said, "It's me. I'm Claudia." Then, she introduced me as her *first mentor* to the other jubilant people from her church. In reality, though, God used Claudia to teach me how much He values every one of his creations and the lengths He will go to seek His lost sheep and extend eternal mercy.

12

MIRRORED

In thinking about admirable individuals I met at ECFA whom I was privileged to live life alongside, I focused solely on those who extended mercy that eternally benefitted others. Quickly, my list grew. I decided to select only four stories to expound upon that express a unique aspect of mercy mirrored.

* * *

LEGACY LEAVERS
Karen & Tom Schlindwein * Mali & Jason Bowling

Karen and Tom Schlindwein co-led a monthly support group for couples experiencing infertility and pregnancy loss. Their personal journey embodied many years of losses and infertility. After a significant time period, they were able to adopt twice. A daughter, Amalie (Mali), and son, Joe, were placed by two selfless birth moms and their families. Instead of forgetting their past struggles and living life as a foursome, they reached out to other childless couples to provide encouragement, support, empathy, and healing and called their ministry the Hope Group. On one occasion, Karen called ECFA and asked if I would be their guest speaker and share information about the agency. The night Karen and I met was only the beginning of an ongoing friendship spanning many decades with innumerable twists, turns, and adventures.

Karen and Tom Schlindwein always place others needs before their own as they mirror the love and compassion of Christ to other hurting people in their families or the community. When Mali was placed for adoption with the couple, Karen gave her word to Lois, Mali's birthmother, that she would provide annual updates and photos. For eighteen years, Karen kept her promise and took time and care to lovingly share Mali's life as it unfolded through photos and a lengthy letter she packaged annually and sent directly to Lois and family. Karen and Tom had no idea the treasure those letters were until Lois became very ill and requested to see Karen, Tom, Mali, and Joe a few months before she died.

Mercy was extended, especially by Mali. Lois experienced the complete forgiveness of Christ, His love, and undeserved mercy. After Mali shared her faith in Christ, Lois no longer feared death or eternity and looked ahead with joy. Lois' family brought out all the safely stored letters that were read and reread over the years. These letters were returned to Mali and Karen and became the content for a book, *Dear Lois: Our Adoption Journey,* that was co-authored by this mom and daughter. The profits from the book became the foundation of a community ministry called Chosen, Inc. (Chosen) that Mali and her husband, Jason, began. God placed a dream in their hearts to open their home and arms to foster children. That ministry has expanded to become a recognized non-profit organization providing fostering and adoption support and education. They extend mercy through the following mission statement: *Chosen exists to foster forever families by living the Gospel so that all children can experience a safe and loving home.*

There are many ways to become involved in this vital ministry as an individual, couple, or even family by going to their website: www.choseninlove.org. Only heaven will reveal how many lives were changed for eternity through this one family who responded each time they received God's direction and mercy in their lives.

* * *

LIFEGIVING LAWYERS
Steve Hayes, Elizabeth Neary, Wendy Gebauer, & Edward Plagemann

Hayes, Neary, Gebauer, and Plagemann has the sound of an experienced law firm, and that would be somewhat accurate. Each of these godly people—Steve, Elizabeth, Wendy, and Ed—have dedicated their lives to coming alongside and representing the courageous individuals of an adoption triad during a difficult legal and emotional process. Their clients often experience a myriad of emotions spiraling downward and upward as tears, both happy and sad, flow freely. The sincere sensitivity and compassion from each of these men and women is generously bestowed to callers seeking advisement and those who become their clients. The results are permanent life changes affecting future generations.

In working cooperatively on hundreds of voluntary termination of parental rights cases with these two separate firms (Grady, Hayes, & Neary LLC and Edward J

Plagemann, Attorney at Law), we all became more than professional associates. During some of the most challenging and impossible situations, we often witnessed God's intervention time after time. I believe this is what deepened and continues to sustain our friendships.

I truly loved every one of my birthparent clients. It was important to me that other professionals treasured them as much as I did. That's why working with both of these law firms was always a joy in the midst of a difficult and painful process. I observed firsthand and appreciated their respect and value for every birthparent making a sacrificial decision to place their baby, twins, or child with an adoptive couple, family, or sometimes relative they carefully, purposely, and even lovingly selected.

When Ed met for legal consult with the birthmothers and sometimes birthfathers prior to the court proceedings of voluntarily terminating their parental rights, he knew I might ask him to lead us in a prayer before we would all walk into the juvenile judge's courtroom. Those were beautiful moments to remember where God's presence and peace filled all our hearts. In my mind, I often thought of another parent by the name of Abraham and his decision of obedience to God to offer his son, Isaac.

Since I was usually in a close relationship of many months or sometimes years with the birthmother or both birthparents, I grieved with them as they'd have to convince the presiding judge of their sound decision in the course of answering 120 questions. These questions were asked by the presiding attorney we hired for that particular case—either Ed, Elizabeth, or Steve. The questions were phrased in accordance with the State of Wisconsin requirements to terminate all of their parental rights so the child could be freed for adoptive placement. The intense process lasted around forty-five minutes to an hour but often seemed like an eternity. After all questioning, the judge would make a decision and strike the gavel in a gesture of formality. Some judges would add personal statements of mercy and empathy to the birthparent or birthparents while others seemed cold and indifferent.

After the hearing was over, orders of termination were signed by the judge, guardian ad litem for the minor child, and our agency attorney. Sobbing afterward in the hallway was the usual norm. Oftentimes, Ed brought along a pocket-sized Gideon Bible he personalized that he gave to the birthparents out in the hall only after the court case concluded. He wanted them to know they could call him at any time in the future about their case or about God's Word too. He cared about their souls and was not ashamed to share his faith if it seemed the client showed interest.

Both Attorney Steve Hayes and Paralegal Wendy Gebauer received an Angel in Adoption Honoree Award in 2005 and 2014, respectively. This prestigious award has been given annually since 1999 to one or two from each state by the Congressional Coalition Adoption Institute (CCAI) at a gala event held in Washington, D.C. It is said to be the most inspiring event of the year for Congress members that always has cooperative bipartisan participation. Together, participants of the CCAI honor the extraordinary efforts of individuals, couples, or organizations who work tirelessly to affect change in the field of adoption, permanency, and child welfare. In my life, these four individuals should receive the Mercy Extended Without Judgement Award for selflessly serving others without reservation.

* * *

LIFESAVERS
Jill & Dan Hait

Another precious person in my life who came to settle in chilly Wisconsin from sunny California is Jill Hait. She initially responded to a tiny classified ad for an adoption program supervisor for our agency in 2003. When I called her to come in for an interview, her voice expressed a warmth, tenderness, and sincerity that would be key in connecting with prospective adoptive couples and families.

In the interview, she humbly shared that a few years before coming to Wisconsin, she shared an idea and passion she had with her former boss, Wayne Tesch, an assistant pastor. Jill envisioned a unique camping program in California specifically for children in foster care. Her idea came to fruition and was named Royal Family KIDS. The mission today is to create positive, life-changing moments for innocent children who have been victims of neglect, abuse, and abandonment. Today, these camp programs exist in every state across America and in nine countries worldwide.

Jill was hired and began her season of thirteen years at ECFA, expressing an unlimited amount of love, mercy, and patience toward prospective adoptive couples and especially the children.

My friendship with Jill grew quickly at ECFA as so many unique situations involving adoption (domestic and international), foster care, birthparents, investigation, court hearings, events, real stories, laughter, tears, lots of prayers, and some crazy inquiry calls became the substance of our daily lives. We saw firsthand how God worked miracles in impossible situations. Quite often, we encouraged each other when difficult circumstances became overwhelming in work and our personal lives too. As the years went by, we could anticipate what the next sentence would be from each other before words were ever spoken. Most importantly, we grew in our faith and trust in God.

On the home front, Jill, her husband, Dan, and stepson, Ben, participated together in a Royal Family KIDS camp in 2011 held in Wisconsin not far from their home, which lit the fire for her and her family to consider becoming a foster family. It was a unique experience for all of them to have a home study done. Jill skillfully completed home studies for hundreds of other couples at ECFA. Being on the other end was definitely a stretching and sometimes stressful process they weathered.

Then, years later, one afternoon following a long meeting and training at our corporate ECFA office in Wheaton, Illinois, I was already seated in the car with my seat belt snuggly buckled. Jill said she needed to have a quick conversation or two and would be out momentarily. I always had emails, texts, and calls to return, so I didn't mind the quiet moments to catch up on a few things. The car's back door opened as Jill placed some files, her purse, a carrying bag, and jacket in the back seat. I looked at Jill as she put on her driving glasses ready to drive both of us back for a two-and-a half-hour return trip. Conversations always flowed so easily between us. We usually stopped for a quick bite at the drive-thru of Portillo's hot dogs, which were simply the best-tasting Chicago-style dogs anywhere. She looked so serious, and I actually played over in my mind the next unexpected statements that seemed to be shared in slow-motion.

Jill said she had met with Ken, our executive director, to let him know that during the meeting we attended, she felt God's prompting to take her own advice. She knew she needed to leave her position at the agency to be a stay-at-home mom. Ken's response was "does Linda know?" Jill said because she was in Illinois at the moment, she felt it only right to tell him first before she told me on our drive back home. He was sad to lose such a vital person who always went above and beyond for each of her clients but understood the importance of her supporting Dan and being more available to their sons' needs and development.

As a co-worker, I grieved over losing her as a staff member; however, as a close friend, I was so happy for her decision to be the mom she always wanted to be. She waited for so many years for God to make this a reality through the gift of a godly marriage followed by the opportunities and timing for family foster care and adoption.

Jill utilized all of her skills and resources as a social worker right at home. She and her husband also realized God had given them His mercy years before in the midst of their own heartache and pain before uniting them in marriage. As a couple, He chose and equipped them to be the forever family for two great kids who are becoming young men of godly character who also needed to experience God's eternal mercy in their lives.

Two favorite truths Jill often shared with others were 1) God never makes mistakes and 2) God is always the perfect matchmaker. She saw God become the lifesaver, redeemer, and restorer of broken hearts and in the lives of young and old, both professionally and personally.

* * *

LABORERS & LAUNCHERS
Deane and Ruth Valkenaar

After settling in as a full-time pregnancy support social worker at ECFA in 1995, I became acquainted with a unique resource that provided loving residential care for pregnant young moms and their additional children. The Genesis House of Southeastern Wisconsin truly was a home of new beginnings for each of the residents. Weekly chores were assigned and shared between the residents to instill responsibility and discipline that was often lacking in their upbringing. Meal preparation was also a component taught to the women, providing some interesting experiments and unique memories. Budgeting was implemented, Bible study encouraged, and job preparation practiced. Ideally, residents who followed the rules could stay throughout their pregnancy and an additional six months post-delivery to make certain they could confidently parent and live on their own.

The founders, directors, and full-time houseparents were Deane and Ruth Valkenaar. This couple was the perfect combination to minister, encourage, challenge, and direct each young woman from fourteen to twenty-six who became a long-term resident.

Deane was always fair, firm, yet fatherly as he desired the very best outcome and future for every resident in their care. He was very pastoral to advise the residents without being harsh and always prayed for them even after they left. Deane always presented options, resources, and probable consequences to residents in their decision-making to encourage each young woman to begin making better choices.

Ruth nurtured the young women as a mother, became an exemplary teacher, and showed empathy for the symptoms of pregnancy and post-delivery. She was often the labor coach at the hospital since many residents were estranged from their families. For many, Ruth was the only positive female in their lives. Her gentleness and wisdom were priceless gifts she freely shared with the women, *her girls*, to hopefully pass onto their newborns if they chose to parent. After delivery and return to the Genesis House, Ruth helped the new moms bond with their babies instead of the popular behavior to pass around their babies to others for holding, feeding, and diaper-changing.

I truly appreciated their selfless example as a husband and wife, pseudo dad and mom, and ministry partners. They were an authentic example of God's unconditional love and unlimited mercy in the community and behind closed doors in the Genesis House.

Whenever they invited me to come to the Genesis House, I explored the option of adoption with those residents who didn't feel ready to become full-time moms. Many residents who were in the midst of their first pregnancy personally observed the challenges of the moms and newborns and realized the magnitude of commitment and responsibility involved in parenthood. Deane and Ruth knew my style and always trusted me to counsel the women with all options, including parenting, temporary foster or relative care, or adoption.

Quite a few of the resident moms lovingly chose the option of adoption for their babies. Some were open adoptions and have been able to reconnect with their birth children and the adoptive parents in endearing relationships through the years. Others have chosen to pray for opportunities to reconnect. A number of the moms have stayed in contact with me as I appreciate these treasured lifelong friendships.

One day in 1998, Deane called and asked if I could meet with him the following day at a well-known truck-stop restaurant. His tone was serious and to the point. Being the ever-frugal director, he added, "And if you are really hungry, I'll pay for your food too." That was Deane—humorous, yet genuine. I definitely had no idea what he needed to discuss. Ruth had to stay back with the residents, and he was concerned the discussion might be overheard by the residents on site, which he did not want to happen.

The following afternoon, I walked in and saw Deane seated at a table in deep thought. The restaurant was quite empty at the time. He stated the homemade soups were the best, so I ordered one. After praying for our meal and the impending conversation, the smells of the creamy bowl of comfort food already placed at the table wafted through the air. I began to take a sip of the first spoonful of steamy delicious soup. Simultaneously, Deane cleared his throat and began to share how he and Ruth had decided together to move from Wisconsin to Missouri to be closer to some family members after much prayer and discussion.

At this point, he had something in his closed hand that he proceeded to place in my hand. Hmmm … connected metal objects filled my hand as I looked down intently. A wad of keys? But why? I became totally overwhelmed with an explanation he shared. He and Ruth decided to give me the keys to the Genesis House ministry on two conditions. 1) If I agreed to continue their ministry as the director and 2) never sell the property. I was speechless as he proceeded with their reasons why, knowing all three of us loved each and every client served. So many emotions welled up within me as I tried to sort out this unexpected gesture of trust and generosity. I knew it wasn't possible for me to fulfill their request as an employee of ECFA but agreed to pray about the situation and additionally seek guidance from my husband when I got home that evening.

Although that particular plan didn't come to fruition, the Valkenaars founded a Genesis House in Missouri that continues today. They faithfully continued to respond in laboring and launching for the Lord as each door opened. They adopted and raised a son whose very young birthmother had been a longtime resident at the Genesis House. She wanted them to become his adoptive parents after she struggled with life in numerous locations and group homes for a number of years. They agreed after seeking God's confirmation and assurance that they weren't too old to start over with a younger child since their three biological children were now adults.

In August 2008, Deane was named the executive director of the North Central Missouri Chapter of the Red Cross where he served for five years in many roles, including leading and organizing volunteer response teams to many victims of tornadoes, fires, and other disasters in Missouri and other neighboring states.

Deane and Ruth didn't stop with that challenge. Instead, Deane and Ruth applied to SIM Missions in Sudan. They knew their experiences were meant for them to walk deeper in ministry. In applying, Deane shared, "Problem solving is my life's work. I have been working in crisis management most of my adult life. Alleviating suffering has been a passion for many years, and I have worked in many areas in order to accomplish this goal. Physical, emotional, and spiritual suffering must be addressed in order to help the person heal." As a result, he and Ruth left the states in September 2013 after training, orientation, and fundraising for personal financial support to serve a number of unreached people groups. They grew very close to the local people and saw a tremendous amount of spiritual growth and leadership in this area of hostility and constant tribal conflict.

Unexpectedly, in 2016, Deane was asked to become the SIM Sudan country director, but he didn't feel qualified to accept the position. Once again, he and Ruth sought God's mercy, grace, and counsel through scripture. They openly consulted with their four adult children, grandchildren, and close friends. After a few months, he willingly accepted the position for which God already knew he was qualified.

Deane and Ruth witnessed how God's hand and presence was present in daily ways as conversions to Christianity and discipleship commitments multiplied. On Christmas Day in 2016, a country war broke out a few yards from where Deane had shared the Christmas message a few hours earlier with hundreds who attended. He and Ruth, although not targets, hid for two days on the floor of their tiny abode hearing bullets fire. An airplane was dispatched from Kenya so everyone on the team could be airlifted out on December 27, 2016. The results were devastating with lives lost and homes ravaged. Despite the trials, Deane and Ruth returned after a few months when some of the country tension quelled. They established new goals and focuses. Then, little by little, people who had been hiding bravely returned to find out more about Jesus and get baptized.

Another challenge was presented to Deane and Ruth in 2018 that would become life-changing. Symptoms that mimicked ALS began to impede Deane's daily responsibilities. His daughter who is a physician in Washington insisted her dad receive a second opinion from her hospital. She was correct that he did not have ALS and was conclusively diagnosed with Isaac's Syndrome, an extremely rare autoimmune disease with ongoing pain and symptoms. She researched the infusion treatments that may provide some minimal relief for his pain and progression. Reluctantly, in July 2019, Deane and Ruth returned permanently back to the US.

Deane and Ruth remain intentional to find joy in each day and haven't stopped laboring for and launching new Christians wherever they reside. As SIM's country director of Sudan, Deane continues to lead virtually and gleans insight from many of his favorite verses found in the Book of Job.

* * *

Each of these twelve life-changers highlighted in this chapter continue to mirror mercy and extend the gift to eternally impact the futures of others throughout their world.

13

MCINTYRED

Over sixty years ago, a baby named Brian and another named Debbie were born within a few days of each other in Michigan and Kansas. These two met each other in 1978 at Grand Rapids School of the Bible and Music and ultimately fell in love. Their lives would traverse through many adventures, including getting married, welcoming the birth of twins, answering a call to the pastorate, discovering what youth ministry entails, planting and shepherding a church, becoming a foster family, committing to adopt a first, second, and third time, beginning an overseas ministry, experiencing the deep sacrifice of the death of a teen-aged son, and receiving a cancer diagnosis.

Brian and Debbie McIntyre are an authentic couple who experience God daily by joining Him in what He is already doing. They've discovered what eternal mercy and true worship is all about. Their life theme has been extending God's mercy to others even when it seems absolutely impossible.

Brian, Debbie, and their twins had approached ECFA in the early 1990s to volunteer as a foster family after the

ECFA director, Ralph Story, presented the work of the agency at the church they attended. They became state licensed to care for two babies or children through age two and had provided short term care for a number of infants in their home. They knew this was a ministry God equipped their family to provide.

I was introduced to the McIntyre family of four by my supervisor, Ron, shortly after I began employment as a social worker at ECFA. I needed to request their services as a foster family for a cute little toddler with dark blonde tousled hair. His young single mom, Rhonda, was on my initial caseload. She had two children under the age of four, and he was her youngest. Rhonda and her mother became overwhelmed with trying to balance school, work, health issues, and limited finances. The request was made to place the youngest child for some extended temporary foster care. He was the connection for me to meet the McIntyres because they were available for the requested months to provide him consistent care. They invited Rhonda and her family to their home so Rhonda's mom and the other sibling would be comfortable knowing the layout of the home, and they'd also get to meet the family who was caring for her son. Rhonda gathered all of her little boy's clothing and favorites, including a blanket, stuffed animal, cup, and even a few snack items for a smooth transition.

When we all arrived at the McIntyre's, I was immediately aware how nurturing and gentle Debbie was and the sense of humor and spontaneity that Brian displayed. The twins were so respectful and patient with this little guy and quite helpful in response to their parents' requests. The interaction among all of them with each other was absolutely beautiful despite the many emotions that were present. That temporary placement was the beginning of a plan God began that day eventually leading to his adoption. A few years later, two more children also became siblings to the twins. In all three of the adoptions, it definitely amazed me to see Brian and Debbie respond with grace and mercy to God's next call of obedience and challenge in their lives.

Their unwavering faith and fervent hope in Christ including what was unseen continued. For approximately ten years, Brian pastored a Bible-based church in Wisconsin that ministered to a number of uniquely called families who fostered and adopted children of all ages and races. Then, God placed a new vision and a dream within Brian and Debbie. It was a passion to minister to terminally ill, abused, and abandoned children in the distant land of West Africa.

The McIntyres founded a ministry in 2004 called West African Mercy Ministries (WAMM). Brian's focus centered on that ministry, resulting in wise planning to step away from his church as the lead pastor. A number of like-minded people wholeheartedly agreed with Brian and Debbie's vision and mission and also came on board. The uncharted waters of beginning a ministry in Accra, Ghana, West Africa, required patience, trust, wisdom, and multiple lessons to navigate through the difficult first years. Recognizing there was a tremendous need to serve the babies and children fueled them when they felt discouraged. God always provided exactly the person, finances, or miracle needed at exactly the right moment and not a day before.

The first phase was to open a children's HOMe, which is actually an acronym for House of Mercy. This initial facility was opened in 2010 and provides hospice care and housing specifically for the young children and babies who are terminally ill, abused, or abandoned. Referrals come from the hospitals, police, and community who are aware of the quality loving care provided to the frailest in society. Since WAMM's inception, the goal and dream were to never turn any child away in need of care. A strategic detailed business plan stressing the importance of relying always upon God's direction first and foremost can be viewed online at https://www.westafricanmercy.org.

Since 2010, ten children who were cared for at HOMe were legally placed for adoption with couples and families from the United States and various countries. However, the option for out of country adoption has changed. Law changes in Ghana since 2018 made all out-of-country adoptions more difficult, making future placements unlikely. The unfortunate result was that some children and babies were turned away because there were no longer any cribs or room available. The majority of the children at HOMe will remain permanently in the care of the loving staff and home parents, Pastor William and Priscilla. The current space is limited to only ten. The majority of the children in HOMe care have severe medical needs requiring daily care. Most local Ghanaian people don't have the financial means to adopt through Ghanaian courts or provide the necessary medications, operations, therapies, and other needs the children may require throughout their lives. However, through WAMM in the HOMe residence, each child without exception is loved, cared for, and provided mercy during their stay. The plan is for a larger facility to be completed on the purchased property that will serve as a model of a Christ-centered foster-family community.

Little by little, God has brought this beloved ministry before the eyes and ears of merciful people around the globe who want to minister in a variety of ways and make an eternal difference in the lives of babies, children, villages, communities, cities, and countries one soul at a time. Personally, I felt an irresistible tug to take a trip and actually visit and serve alongside the WAMM team on the ground in Accra, Ghana, before I began to write the first chapter of this book. I also knew I wanted to give a portion of the proceeds from all book sales to support the works of WAMM.

The first highlight began the following day after a brief night of sleep at the hospitable SIM Christian guesthouse where I would stay the next week. Brian definitely knew how to safely prepare the locally sourced meal ingredients into wonderful-tasting food and also make certain all drinking water was filtered. Brian and Debbie briefed three of us—Tom and Donna, a lovely older married couple originally from a supporting church in Virginia, and me. We were all naïve WAMM mission travelers, and they prepared us for our morning visit to HOMe where we would meet, play, interact, and love on the ten little residents. No preparation could have completely addressed all the emotions that surfaced and natural reactions during our first visit. Joy, tears, laughter, empathy, hope, faith, wonder, silliness, unworthiness, adrenalin highs, compassion, gratitude, and an overwhelming inadequacy were all part of our first day. We were filled with an immense desire to return and provide respite care for Pastor William and Priscilla to enjoy a fun date lunch together without children to care for or soothe. Reluctantly, they said they would consider the offer.

Ten children quickly captured our hearts that day. These children are part of the twenty-three long-term placed children of HOMe ministry. The diagnoses of the ten we were blessed to hold, feed, pray for, and play with included: HIV 3, autism, stroke, cardiac issues, cerebral palsy, developmentally delayed, physically delayed, stroke, hydrocephalus, and failure to thrive. The Ghanaian women who are hired to help with feeding, laundry changes, cooking, cleaning, and medical care were also delightful to get to know and appreciate. Prosper, the HOMe and WAMM driver, was employed to transport the children to school, all medical appointments, and wherever else he was asked to drive. He was also fully invested in the well-being of each child. It was so obvious to the three of us visitors how much each child is loved and cared for regardless of their ability to respond.

In Accra, the vision and mission of WAMM continues outside the walls and security gate of HOMe to serve many children in the Yam Market area of Agbogbloshie. The market area is home to a largely populated slum of makeshift dwellings that surround the capitol city garbage dump. A trickling unfiltered water stream weaves between the dirt paths and rows of shacks that house numerous family members. Many people take shifts sleeping on hard dirt floors, watching out for one another from doorless abodes while earning meager incomes from selling their yams and trash finds.

Every Saturday, Pastor William and his dedicated team of six to eight godly young men and women gather in the empty public school building with over a hundred children of all ages from the Yam Market Agbogloshie slum area. The children attend his program voluntarily for three hours and often bring their siblings, relatives, and neighbors. Pastor William's energetic team works full time at their places of employment during the week, then willingly share their Saturday to present applicable scripture lessons, lively songs, formal school preparedness, opportunities to earn points to go to school or Christian retreats, and a small snack.

Tom and I were invited to be a part of this outreach that truly changed me and inspired me to partner with Pastor William and the team for some future ministries for those beautiful children of that location. Donna was not feeling well and stayed at the guesthouse to rest. These loving children sung worship songs in their language, and some sung in English, creating an angelic surreal sound that caused emotion to surface in me and also Tom. We were awestruck by the hunger in the children to learn and recite God's Word and delight themselves in the music of praise and worship to God.

Tom and I were both asked to share a separate devotion with all of the children that morning. Without consulting one another, we discovered both of our messages tied seamlessly to each other's and then to Pastor William's scripture about the Good Shepherd from John 10:11. When we took our turns to share, an interpreter translated for the many children who only spoke and understood Twi, which is one of over thirty languages spoken in Ghana.

I took photos and some video footage on my cell phone when the children sang. When I carefully peered through my pictures that evening, the face of one young girl seemed to capture the essence of true worship and communing with her merciful Jesus.

I have looked at her face this past year when struggling to write a section or chapter of this book. She reminds me of the importance of finishing and sharing the message behind *Mercy Extended*. She inspires me to take the next steps to share the opportunity for other readers and listeners to continue the vital spiritual and practical ministry to her and the other children of the Yam Market today and tomorrow. This type of missional ministry is eternally focused for all those currently living in West Africa and those who will be in the future.

The McIntyres answered the call to go when they first heard about it, and they humbly joined God in all the aspects of this ministry. One of the young men who Brian discipled in Accra for years became a Pastor and is shepherding a little flock of new Christians in a hilly populated area with his beautiful wife who leads the worship time. I was awestruck how everyone at the church wore beautiful clothing for the service. One of the ladies shared with me that they are there to worship God and want to give Him their first time of the week and wear their very nicest clothing. A lovely teen at church who sang loudly and praised God unashamedly with all her heart came up to me after the service smiling and introduced herself. She said her name with a little accent that I didn't quite understand, so I asked her if she could spell it. Slowly, she said, "Yes, madame, I will spell it for you. It is: M-E-R-C-Y." All I could say was "I truly love your name, which has so much meaning." She giggled and hugged me, and I thanked God for another amazing part of journeying with the McIntyres.

14

MULTIPLIED & MAXIMIZED

After returning from Accra, Ghana, my plans to immediately begin writing were shelved. I became very ill on my last flight back and couldn't be diagnosed accurately for a period of time since many things had to first be ruled out. It seems I had an adverse reaction to one of the many vaccines I needed to have before traveling to the African continent. Prior to my departure, God provided Dr. Joyce Sanchez, a wonderful travel and infectious disease specialist, for me.

At the initial visit, she provided exceptional travel counsel and appropriate prescriptions to stay medically safe and well. Upon returning, she availed herself to treat me since I was between primary physicians. She graciously stayed with me for months to share her wisdom, order appropriate tests, extend medical care, show her unconditional compassion, share her sweet godly spirit, engage in ongoing prayer for me, and encourage me when I needed it. All were the perfect combination to get me through a challenging time when extreme fatigue, a full neurological system compromise, and decrease in cognition were daily experiences from mid-February until the beginning of June when every symptom was finally gone.

Most days during that season, post-Ghana, I had a more difficult time reading and comprehending. Before the trip, Mike carefully copied and pasted numerous scripture verses relating specifically to the topic of mercy on seven pages he stapled together for me. I originally packed them in my carry-on so I could frequently refer to them wherever I was during my mercy-immersion trip. While recovering, I held tight to these pages. The verses became my strength and encouragement. My favorite verse was from Lamentations 3:22–23 (ESV). *"The steadfast love of the Lord never ceases; his mercies never come to an end; they are new every morning; great is your faithfulness."* It made my soul and spirit feel very strengthened even when other parts of me were not as strong. Through a few months of physical weakness, I began to grasp the depth and magnitude of that relevant and powerful scripture. Mercy that originates from God is new and fresh every day and is given without limit because it is a gift and more so because God is faithful.

Scripture is clear, and God is faithful even when we are not. At some point, we may become more aware life is not about us and what can make us happy. This occurs when we become selfless instead of self-centered and recognize we were created by our Creator who desires a relationship with each person. Our purpose for existence will become obvious, exciting, authentic, and fulfilled. Our souls become ignited and may begin to attract the interest and pique the curiosity of other souls hardened by hypocrisy, false teachings, hurt, rejection, and a host of other reasons unique to each person. It's so exciting to see a person's transformation after they receive the gift of mercy extended.

This past year, our church, Grace Baptist in Waukesha, Wisconsin, witnessed the visible and internal change of a sixty-four-year-old man named Ron. He had been incarcerated for thirty-three years and was a member of the Outlaws Motorcycle Club. When he was released from prison, he was placed in a halfway house two doors away from a wonderful family—Matt and Angie and their daughter, Karis. They were members from our church who had been missionaries for nineteen years to tribal people groups in Papua, New Guinea. One day, both Matt and Ron took their garbage containers to the curb at the same time and exchanged greetings.

An unlikely friendship quickly developed between them. Meals together, heart-to-heart conversations, laughter, and kindness resulted in Ron's heart surrender to Jesus. During this period, Ron began attending church with Matt's family for the first time in his life. He knew the first day he visited that he was accepted and loved by everyone. Being forgiven by God and starting life anew was quite visible in Ron's appearance, demeanor, and even his language. He began inviting others to church from his sphere of influence and community group he was required to be part of as a condition of his parole.

Ironically, Ron's physical health began to decline swiftly in contrast to his rapid spiritual growth and hunger for God's Word. He was diagnosed with emphysema and other lung conditions, which impacted him significantly.

Eight months after wholly submitting to following God, Ron—aided by a walker and portable oxygen tank—was helped to the front of church. He wanted to share his personal testimony of new life in Jesus. He began his story with the heartache of being abandoned as a young boy by his mother who became the property of the Outlaws and raised by his biological father who held a leadership position in the Outlaws. His warped sense of normalcy led to a life of crime, drugs, an extensive record, and ultimately, a three-decade-plus prison sentence, which he served and survived by maintaining his facade of a tough and hardened guy.

He realized after he met his personable neighbors and watched how they interacted with one another that he wanted whatever they had. Ron knew they genuinely cared about him but why? It was time to stop running and acknowledge his deep need for God's mercy and grace.

At the podium, he spoke about the newfound joy, peace, and love from God that abounded in him and his desire to be kind, thoughtful, and encouraging toward others. He knew God fully forgave him of every wrong-doing he did. Ron, in turn, wanted to forgive his family and others for hurting him. There weren't many dry eyes after Ron concluded his story that day. Then, in July 2019, right before his sixty-fourth birthday, Ron was baptized. He lived longer than his doctor had initially thought, and Ron wanted to make a public declaration of his soul-transformation. His neighbor, Matt, and Pastor Doug shared in the honor. Each day, while Ron continues to live, he prays for other people who may be struggling physically, spiritually, or emotionally.

A natural by-product of internal soul-transformation possible only through Jesus should be an overwhelming desire to serve, give, forgive, and extend mercy and grace in abundance to others without any reciprocity. It is the outward proof or demonstration of what has taken place within. The fact is faith alone is dead. Deeds or actions completed apart from faith are good but lack eternal value. When one's faith in Jesus becomes coupled with actions, then eternal results naturally follow:

- Lives are transformed
- Generations are impacted
- Multitudes become mobilized

… for eternity.

I have watched faith in Christ grow in my precious family as lives are transformed, future generations are impacted, and multitudes of people and communities are mobilized throughout the world. In God's economy, I've seen how He multiplies and maximizes puny human efforts, uses a timeline unlike ours, and loves when we trust Him with the impossible so we realize it's Him at work and not us. Yet He still chooses to patiently invite us to join Him in what He is already doing and allow people to reach and connect to other people as mercy is extended from God first and then through you and me.

> For we are His workmanship, created in Christ Jesus for good works, which God prepared beforehand, that we should walk in them.
>
> —Ephesians 2:10 (ESV)

MERCY MOMENT OF TRUTH

During an appointed season in everyone's life, soul-searching begins. Internal questions begin to interrupt thoughts quietly at first and then louder and louder. It is how our loving Creator designed us. We become curious as to why and for what purpose we are created. Realization of the unique differences in each person becomes more apparent. Age, status, nationality, gender, and race make no difference in this pursuit for answers and ultimate truth. The pilgrimage is universal.

Seeking answers, experimenting, and finding temporary self-centered solutions apart from truth may lead us in many confusing directions. This often results in discontentment, discouragement, and dead ends.

Philosophies, disciplines, theories, metaphysical beliefs, cults, and more become soul distractions that lure and then rob us of a transformed life found only through a personal relationship with God.

Truth Treasure:

And you were dead in the trespasses and sins in which you once walked, following the course of this world, following the prince of the power of the air, the spirit that is now at work in the sons of disobedience—among whom we all once lived in the passions of our flesh, carrying out the desires of the body and the mind, and were by nature children of wrath, like the rest of mankind. But God, being rich in mercy, because of the great love with which he loved us even when we were dead in our trespasses, made us alive together with Christ—by grace you have been saved—and raised us up with him and seated us with him in the heavenly places in Christ Jesus, so that in the coming ages he might show the immeasurable riches of his grace in kindness toward us in Christ Jesus. For by grace you have been saved through faith. And this is not your own doing; it is the gift of God, not a result of works, so that no one may boast.

—Ephesians 2:1–9 (ESV)

In this declarative passage of scripture, the bleak and hopeless state of every person born on this earth is clearly and unequivocally described. It is devastating to fathom the depth and sobering reality that we are spiritually dead and separated from God through our transgressions and sins, even though our bodies may be alive. Our choice to follow the god of this world aka devil/Satan leaves only one alternative when we physically die—the just sentencing to an eternity of hell.

BUT GOD who is rich in mercy and grace extends His unmerited gift of eternal life through Jesus Christ to each and every person who puts their faith and trust in Him. The destiny-affecting decision however is left up to each individual until their last heartbeat and final breath. Our salvation is the sole reason Jesus the Savior knew His purpose for being born. He lived thirty-three years on this earth experiencing the same trials and temptations we do. In love, He chose to fully surrender Himself to horrific physical pain, emotional turmoil, and total abandonment from God, family, and His closest friends prior to death. His life was and is the only acceptable payment for every single sin and transgression of humanity, whether in thought, word, or action; past, present, or future. Simply stated, one is either hell-bound or heaven-bound.

Only One Question on The Quest Remains

- Have you ever considered your purpose in life and ultimate destiny?

My Response/Your Response

I have. When given the opportunity, I chose to accept the mercy extended while seated in the middle of a busy restaurant with a man who took time to care where I would spend the rest of my eternity.

* My heart was open
* The truth of God's Word shared
* My own sinfulness undeniable, and
* An insatiable desire in that moment of time for a new beginning or birth.

Today, before this book concludes, realize **I care deeply where you will spend your eternity.**

* If your heart is open
* The truth of God's Word stirs within you
* You recognize your own sinfulness and unworthiness
* Yearning for a new start, birth, and transformed life is your desire at this moment …

… then simply talk to God.

Mercy ♥ Extended

For God so loved the world, that He gave His only Son, that whoever believes in Him should not perish but have eternal life. For God did not send His Son into the world to condemn the world, but in order that the world might be saved through Him.
—John 3:16–17 (ESV)

Let Him know you accept the mercy extended to you by Jesus. Invite Him to take soul residence. Believe He is able to forgive all your past, present, and future sins. Get ready for a new life forgiven and free—with a clear direction and purpose you were created to live.

* If you have made that choice today, contact me at: OberbrunnerLinda@gmail. com so we can rejoice together! Some helpful free resources for your next steps will be shared, if desired.

NOTES

Chapter 4—Matched
1) The Mexican Hat Dance or Jarabe Tapatio performed by first graders can be found at https://www.youtube.com/watch?v=qvRRvMw9-fg. In comparison, professional Mexican dancers perform this national dance with more style, flair, and elegance. You can watch that video at https://www.youtube.com/watch?v=QN-p4mUbq6k. The night Mike and I first met during this dance, we definitely looked more like the first graders example.

Chapter 9—Missioned
1) The poem by Sandra Higgs is reprinted with permission from *Alliance Life Magazine*, January 18, 1989.

Chapter 10—Ministered
1) Chick tracts are defined as small hand-sized cartoon gospel stories that people love to read. They are printed in over 100 languages and have sold over 900 million tracts in the first 50 years. The first tract was self-published in 1960 by founder Jack Chick who died in 2016. There are over 250 different titles and additional evangelistic products for people to share the gospel. For more information, visit their website at https://www.chick.com.

ACKNOWLEDGMENTS

GOD—for extending mercy
so you and I can experience His unmerited grace & favor.

***

I am so grateful for the many people who have been
an integral part of my life and the birthing of this book.

My parents, Dan & Ginny, brothers, Danny, and John
(Nancy), and baby sister, Mary Catherine.

Godparents: Marion W. and Clarence S.

My husband and best friend, Mike.

Our precious children and their valued spouses: Kim,
Kary (Kelly), Sarah, and Jeremy (Lachelle); and treasured
grandkids: Keegan, Isabel, Addison, Hannah, Josiah, and
Jordan.

Family relatives (hundreds) and In-laws: Millie and Bucko,
Bill and Darlene, Ken and Linda, aunts, uncles, cousins—1st, 2nd, and 3rd—nieces, nephews, and more.

My dearest friends (hundreds), beginning with Jan from grade school, Mercy High School, neighbors, church family friends, ministry/employment life connections, prayer partners, and past clients who all became close and have stayed connected.

John Fisco, my spiritual father—deceased February 9, 2020.

African mission trip supporters and encouragers.

West African Mercy Ministries (WAMM) leadership and staff—ongoing sacrificial service.

Inspiring children of Ghana whose smiles, greetings, and hugs remain permanently in my heart.

Women's Bible Study faithfuls of past & present sharing the WORD—Women's Aglow leaders: Fay K and Kay B; home study leader: Debbie M.; and MFM Ministries: Margo F.

The Excellent Author Academy Elite Team: Outstanding Editor Tina Morlock, Nanette O'Neal; Mark and Shelly Photography; Frank & Cheryl Kendralla; Crissy Maier, and Felicity Fox.

Igniting Souls Superior Support from Chief Igniter, Kary Oberbrunner, and entire Tribe.

Martyn Wood for prayerfully acknowledging the book and dream within me.

For lifelong cheerleaders and encouragers: Bob C., Danice C., Eileen C., Kit G., Wendy G., Carl & JoAnne M., Ann & Irv P., Beth R., Nancy S., Carol & Don T. and Jim & Leah V.

Humble & faithful prayer intercessors & warriors.

Author Stormie Omartian, whose inspirational books transformed my prayer life as a young mom and wife.

All the individuals who have allowed me to share your stories to bring *Mercy Extended* to life so others will have the opportunity to understand why *Mercy Extended* is the gift that transforms lives, impacts generations, and mobilizes multitudes for eternity.

Got a story inside you?

Author Academy Elite could be the right choice for helping you write, publish, and market your book.

Discover more at:

http://bit.ly/MercyExtended